Thomas Leffingwell

The Connecticut Pioneer
Who Rescued
Chief Uncas and the Mohegans

by

Russell Mahan

Published by Historical Enterprises
Historical Enterprises@Outlook.com

First Edition: September 2018
Printed in the United States of America
ISBN: 9780999396223

All photographs and illustrations are individually credited;
those without credit are by the author.
The words "The Bravery of Lieut. Thomas Leffingwell"on the cover
are a detail of the Leffingwell Monument on the Mohegan Reservation.
The signature of Thomas Leffingwell is
from a 1685 survey description.

Thomas Leffingwell

The Connecticut Pioneer Who Rescued Chief Uncas and the Mohegans

Table of Contents

Introduction

What first drew my attention to Thomas Leffingwell was the fact that he was a personal friend of the great Mohegan chief Uncas, and had rescued him and his people in their hour of peril from Narragansett enemies. This daring deed raised the suggestion by genealogical author Dr. Albert Leffingwell (1845-1916) that perhaps Thomas Leffingwell was the prototype, the living inspiration, for the fictional character called Hawkeye in the book *The Last of the Mohicans* and Natty Bumppo in *The Deerslayer*. I wondered whether this was true. What is the actual story of this man?

These questions were what initially drew me to look into the details of the life of Thomas Leffingwell. It is easy for later descendants to attribute grand accomplishments to their ancestors so they can bask in the reflected glory of their achievements. But what is the historical evidence, as opposed to the historical wish? This question shall be considered throughout the course of this work.

Thomas Leffingwell led an interesting, full and long life. Three hundred and fifty years later, he is still well known in Norwich. It is true that he lived among the Mohegans and was a friend of their famous chief Uncas, but he was much more than that. He was present at the creation of Connecticut, from the first frontier days with the Native Americans in the 1630s to the 1710s as a settled and established colony of England. He lived in America in the days before there were Americans, when colonists happily considered themselves to be English.

Reconstructing the life of a person who lived nearly four hundred years ago is a work of art in the sense that it must be reasonably imagined based upon the recorded facts. Much information is irretrievably lost, so gaps must be filled in with likelihoods and probabilities based upon background information. Unfortunately, Leffingwell kept no personal diary which has survived. There were no newspapers in Connecticut during his lifetime, so events that would have been chronicled in a local paper went unrecorded. No history of Connecticut in book form was written until the late 1700s, long after he had departed the scene. Nevertheless, a rich life still emerges.

A few introductory matters about this book need to be mentioned.

English calendars and English spelling during the life of Thomas Leffingwell are both familiar to us now and yet different. In those days England and its colonies operated on the old Julian calendar, which had the same months of the year as the modern Gregorian system. However, the year started on March 25th, not January 1st. This was because the Christian era began with Jesus, whose birth date was observed on December 25th, and whose conception was calculated as having been on March 25th. That day therefore marked the beginning of the new Christian year in the Julian calendar.

This leads to some confusion for us now. December 31, 1637, for example, was followed the next day by January 1, 1637. Three months later, New Year's Eve was March 24, 1637, followed the next morning by New Year's Day, March 25, 1638. Outside of England, most of the rest of Europe was already on the modern calendar. Between January 1 and March 24 the French and Spanish would say it was 1638, but the English would call it 1637. The English were aware even then that they were out of step, and so the manner of indicating the year for dates between January 1st and March 24th under the old calendar was sometimes (but not always) to designate it, for example, as January 7, 1704/1705. This is shown in a detail of a deed by Thomas Leffingwell:

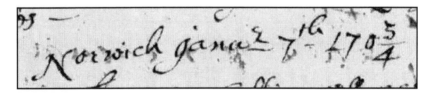

This double year system for dates up to March 24th will be followed in this book.

Often, however, they simply stated the year using their own system, casting a little doubt into what year it really was. Also, because of leap year discrepancies under the Julian system, the two calendars were off by about eleven days. In 1752 England and the colonies joined the Gregorian system, changing New Year's Day to January 1st and adding eleven days to the calendar. After the transition, some dates that had already passed were recalculated under the new calendar. For example, at the time of the event, George Washington was born on February 11, 1731, but this same day was later re-designated as February 22, 1732. The reader should simply be aware that this calendaring situation puts the identification of some years into question.

The English language, in both speaking and writing, presents an interesting historical issue as well. Thomas Leffingwell spoke the English language of the 1600s, which was very similar to our own yet with some variation. Quotations in this book will be in the original spelling of the 1600s except where modification is necessary to clarify the meaning to the modern reader. It should be noted that the spelling of words in those days was not standardized, and people were free to use any assortment of letters they chose to convey the intended sound and meaning. Two people could spell the same word differently, and neither would be wrong. The English language was not made uniform to always spell the same word the same way until the early 1800s when dictionaries became common. The spellings in these old public records is interesting and sometimes amusing, and prove that different spellings do still convey the same word to the reader's mind. Quoting it as written gives a better feel for the times, and for the way it really was.

A great many documents have been examined in the preparation of this work. The archives of the Connecticut State Library, the Connecticut Historical Society, Yale University, the New Haven Historical Society, the Old Saybrook Historical Society, and the Leffingwell House Museum have been searched. Town records in Old Saybrook and Norwich have been consulted. Innumerable online sources have been reviewed in detail, including the old and out of print books available at the historical treasure known as Archive.org. Four especially worthy old books deserve mention: *The Leffingwell Record, 1637-1897*, by Dr. Albert Leffingwell, *History of Norwich, Connecticut*, by Frances Manwaring Caulkins, *Old Houses of the Ancient Town of Norwich, 1660-1800*, by Mary E. Perkins, and *A Complete History of Connecticut* by Benjamin Trumbull. Valuable though their writings are, one must take what these authors say with a certain amount of caution, as they all to some extent fall victim at times to writing in a romantic prose. This is particularly true of Dr. Leffingwell, who was a thoughtful family genealogist more than a historian. We must sort through these works to find the facts as best we can, and build a realistic portrait from there.

Historian Benjamin Trumbull in the 1790s wrote of the early years of Connecticut with some trepidation. "I imagine the earliest times of the colony will be attended with the most difficulty, to collect the facts with sufficient certainty," he stated. "It must be a work of time and indefatigable labor and industry, since it has been so long neglected, and the materials, many of them, almost lost, and others scattered and all need so much care in collecting, time in comparing, and judgment in compiling."[1] That was true then, and is still true today. The certainty of historical facts is often elusive; judgment must fill in the gap.

In 1897 the physician Dr. Albert Leffingwell wrote *The Leffingwell Record, 1637-1897*, an excellent book of genealogy identifying Thomas Leffingwell and his descendants down to that day. It is an exhaustive compilation of the hundreds of his descendants, as well as their marriages and children, over the course of two hundred and sixty years. It contains a summary of Thomas Leffingwell's life, and some very well thought out comments about him. It has been the best source of information available to date. In this book I will attempt to complete a work the estimable doctor did not attempt; that is, to write a full biography of the life of Thomas Leffingwell. In doing so, Dr. Leffingwell's interesting thoughts about Thomas will sometimes be considered.

As a matter of ethics and of some personal pride, it is necessary for me as author to disclose that I am a descendant of Thomas Leffingwell. I am including in the appendix a descendancy of the generations from Thomas Leffingwell to me. This connection is what brought me to learn of his existence, but this book is not a genealogical or family history work. It is a legitimate biography, and applies principles of historical inquiry and analysis. I will be establishing the facts as revealed by history, and what can be reasonably deduced from them.

In considering Thomas Leffingwell, it must be remembered that he was a man of the 1600s, and we must accept him in that context. It would be unfair to him to expect him to be a 21st century man in his thoughts and actions. He pre-dated the Greatest Generation of World War II, the era of Victorian thoughts and conduct, and even the basic American foundational principles such as the United States Constitution with its Bill of Rights and the separation of church and state. He lived in days before modern consumerism when scarcity of goods was the predominant situation, and before industrialization when life was completely agricultural in nature and profoundly quiet. Though living in his day seemed modern to him, those days now seem technologically deprived.

In many human ways, Thomas Leffingwell's life was like ours. He had a spouse and children he loved and cared about, friendships he valued, and working relationships he established. He had to work hard to get by in the wilderness of the New World. He lived in a house, and sought ways to improve his life. It can be said that people are people, then and now, except that that simple proposition is not completely accurate. The mindset in those days, the viewpoint of the people living at the time, and his own frame of reference as they and he interpreted what they experienced in life. Thomas Leffingwell was a 1600s Puritan with a Puritan world view, which affected every aspect of how he perceived the world around him and how he should live his life. We must not impose today's standards and perspectives upon him, but allow him to live his life in his own times, and in the world as he perceived it.

Thomas Leffingwell, by all appearances and with no evidence of a reason to doubt it, had a good life, and was happy with it. Yet everyone's life is not so easy as it is lived out moment to moment. We cannot feel the stress and uncertainty of another person's long ago life, back when the end was not known from the beginning. Thomas Leffingwell went alone into the wilderness of the New World, and lived his life one day at a time, not knowing what would happen next.

THOMAS LEFFINGWELL

THOMAS LEFFINGWELL

THOMAS LEFFINGWELL

Chapter 1

An English Boy Among the Indians

"About the year 1637, only a short time after the first settlement of New England, there appears among the forests of Connecticut a young hunter calling himself Thomas Leffingwell.... He was even at that early day on friendly terms with the Mohegan Indians, and especially with their young chief, Uncas; nor is it improbable, that occasionally he lived among them, acquiring their language and sharing their adventures. Very dim, however, are the glimpses which we then obtain of him. He was gifted, tradition tells us, with unusual physical strength...; he was endowed, as we know, with that courage which does not shrink from the greatest of perils, when danger is the only path to accomplishment...."[2] This folklore-like description, written in 1897 by Dr. Albert Leffingwell of his ancestor, is a fitting introduction to Thomas Leffingwell. Its description is sustained by the facts, as will be seen in this book.

This English boy was alone, without father or mother, on the furthest edge of the American frontier. As Dr. Leffingwell said, Thomas was "a youth without fortune or influence."[3] No English settlers were in that Native American land until a year or two before, and now there were only a handful in scattered locations. How did he get here? How was a boy in the English countryside transfigured into a youth living among the Indians in the wilds of the New World?

The answer is that it is not known for certain where Thomas Leffingwell came from, or why he went to Connecticut, or how it was that he ended up at the side of Uncas. As was said in a talk about him a hundred years ago, "his early history and origin are questions of romance and mystery."[4] The full explanation of it was once known to Leffingwell and his family. Unfortunately his story, fascinating as it would have been then and now, was apparently not written down, and it eventually became lost from living memory. If it was ever reduced to writing, the document has not survived. It is therefore necessary to piece his life together from the scattered facts that are known; yet from that emerges a most interesting life indeed.

In 1637 Leffingwell was just twelve or thirteen years old. This is known from a March 19, 1705, affidavit, which still exists in the records of the New

Haven Historical Society. In it he stated that he was at that time 81 years old. This makes his birth year 1624.[5] However, it must be remembered that under the calendaring system then in effect (described in the Introduction to this book) the date of March 19, 1705, would today be designated the year 1706. That would make Thomas a boy of twelve in 1637.

It is known, because Thomas Leffingwell himself said so, that in 1637 he was in Connecticut with Uncas and the Mohegans. The Norwich historian Frances Manwaring Caulkins wrote in the 1860s that "in his testimony before the Court of Commissioners at Stonington in 1705, he says he was acquainted with Uncas in the year 1637."[6] The document upon which she bases this statement can no longer be found, but may exist in a private collection somewhere. There is ample reason to take Caulkins at her word, and assume without doubt that her statement is true because it was based upon a document she had personally seen. Her book has itself become a part of the historical record.

From England

Other than that he was born in England, it is not definitely known whence Thomas Leffingwell came. There are, however, possible alternative explanations of his origin, one of which seems most likely to be true. Writing a hundred and fifty years after Leffingwell's death, the historian Caulkins offered two different explanations. "Thomas Leffingwell, according to minutes preserved among his descendants," she said, "was a native of Croxhall in England."[7] This would seem to have some credence since it was from old documents held by the family. Unfortunately, where those "minutes" are now is not known, and they cannot be examined.

Yet, even in the 1860s, there was already an alternative story. Caulkins wrote further that "a tradition has obtained in some branches of the family that Thomas Leffingwell came to this country from Yorkshire, at fourteen years of age.... The author [Caulkins] is unable to decide whether these traditions should be ranked as fable or fact." There must have been a doubt by Ms. Caulkins of the veracity of the story, though the source of her uncertainty is not disclosed.

One problem with Leffingwell having come as stated in "the minutes preserved among his descendants" is that there is no identifiable "Croxhall" in England. This was pointed out by Dr. Leffingwell in his book, and it still seems to be true. There is, however, a "Croxall," and within that locality there is a manor called "Croxall Hall." Perhaps "Croxhall" is simply a mistaken version of these other names. Another problem is that Croxall is not in or anywhere near the county of Yorkshire, which is the place of origin remembered by other family members. Dr. Leffingwell in 1897 reported in his work that a friend of his, Reverend E. B. Huntington, went on a genealogical expedition to England and found that there were no records of any Leffingwells in Croxall,[8] and there appear to be no Leffingwell records there even today.

A third alternative explanation of the origins of Thomas Leffingwell is offered by Dr. Leffingwell. It is possible that he was born in the village of White Colne, in Essex County, in eastern England. This possibility is based on a record, found there by Reverend Huntington, of the christening on March 10, 1624, of one "Thomas Leppingwell," the son of Thomas and Alice Leppingwell.[9] That record still exists in the *English Parish Registers, 1538-1997*.

No document establishes beyond doubt that the Thomas Leppingwell born in Essex in 1624 is one and the same as our Thomas Leffingwell in Connecticut in 1637. Yet there is good reason to believe that it is likely. Four points strengthen this probability. First, in the March 1705 deposition, previously mentioned, Leffingwell says he was 81 years old, which coincides perfectly with the March 1624 date. Second, over the years there were a number of Leffingwell families, by various spellings, in the English county of Essex.[10] Among the Leffingwell families there, Thomas was a common first name. Third, the slight variation in the name Leppingwell is not an obstacle. Our Thomas Leffingwell is himself called Leppingwell in several Connecticut records.

The spelling of the name Leffingwell is definite now, and has been for hundreds of years, but it seems that it was not so certain in the 1600s. It should be remembered that the particular and consistent spelling of a word was not as important in those days as we deem it to be now. In addition to the Leppingwell variation, there is the unmistakable occasional spelling by Thomas Leffingwell himself of "Leffingwill." His signature on the 1685 legal description (shown in the front of this book), and the facsimile signature given in the 1859 book *The Norwich Jubilee* both clearly have "will" at the end. In American English the name is pronounced "LEFFingWELL," with an emphasis on the both the first and last syllables. In old Essex English, however, it was likely that the final syllable was a clipped sound of "wul" as in "LEFFingwul." It could have been spelled "will" or "well" and still give the same sound. Ultimately, it was decided by the family to spell it "Leffingwell."

The fourth point in support of Thomas Leffingwell being born in Essex in 1624 is that the records in White Colne show the 1603 baptism of one Michael Leppingwell, also the son of parents named Thomas and Alice. Michael appears, therefore, to be the much older brother of our Thomas. Michael corresponds in name and age to the Michael Leppingwell who appears in colonial Boston, Massachusetts, in 1636. Descendants of Michael Leppingwell had an oral family tradition that they were related to the Connecticut Leffingwells.[11] One of Michael's sons was named Thomas, seemingly in honor of his father. These facts form a coherency which seems to indicate an underlying truth, that Thomas and Michael were connected.

This relationship to Michael Leppingwell also provides an explanation for Thomas getting from England to New England. Thomas Leffingwell probably immigrated to the New World by going with, or to, his brother in Boston. This is not a certainty, as no ship record or other document supports it (or refutes it), but it is a reasonable inference, and no other alternative explanation of how or why he got to America has any support whatsoever. Michael was an actual person, apparently from the extended Leppingwell family in Essex, known to have been in the right place (New England), and at the right time (1636).

Nothing is directly known of Thomas Leffingwell's upbringing in England, but some facts can be reasonably inferred. He surely came from an English Puritan family. He was part of the Puritan migration, and when he arrived in America he stayed among Puritan people and participated in that church all this life. Also, he was comfortably literate, suggesting that he learned to read and write in his youth. There exists a letter from 1667 that clearly demonstrates this, and which will be considered later in this work. Literacy for boys in England at that time was about thirty percent,[12] leading to the conclusion that the family in which he was raised in England was relatively well off financially and in social standing, providing him the opportunity and means to learn to read and write. Thus, a well off Puritan family in Essex was the likely background from which Leffingwell came.

Arrival in the New World

For reasons unknown, Thomas Leffingwell went to America without his parents. Perhaps they died, or simply felt the boy would be better off in the New World. Whatever the actual reason may be, as an adolescent he likely went with, or was sent to live with, his relative Michael Leppingwell in Boston.

Dr. Albert Leffingwell in his book guessed at yet another possible explanation of how Thomas came to America. He speculates that Thomas could have gone directly to Saybrook, Connecticut, in 1637 in the charge of an older married sister whose name is not known, and who possibly soon died, leaving Thomas on this own.[13] As he said, this is only a theory of something that could have happened but with nothing to support it in reality. The Michael Leppingwell connection seems much more solid. The truth is, however, that it is simply not known with certainty, and Thomas Leffingwell could have come to America for some other reason not yet discovered or imagined.

But come to America he did. The arrival of Thomas Leffingwell was part of a swelling tide of English immigrants coming into New England in the 1630s. The "Great Puritan Migration" of this era saw some twenty thousand people leave the religious and political turmoil and limited economic opportunity of England and go to what they hoped would be religious freedom and better circumstances in a new land. These people were mainly Puritans, a group of reformists who wanted to change the Church of England but still work within its organization. By contrast, the earlier Pilgrims of the *Mayflower* were separatists who wanted to completely leave the Church of England and start their own reformed church, unencumbered by the ecclesiastical authorities in London. Of course, every person who left the homeland did so for his own individual reasons, and had his own distinctive hopes for a better life.

Many ship records and passenger lists from the 1630s have survived, but not all. Unfortunately, the ship manifests with the names of Michael Leppingwell and Thomas Leffingwell no longer exist. It is not known on which ship or ships they traveled, or when they arrived. It was probably in, or within a year of, 1636.

The crossing of the Atlantic to Massachusetts was both tedious and harrowing. Immigrant ships were crowded and unsanitary, throwing together a mix of people for a slow crossing of the ocean. The ship *Planter*, for example, left London on April 2, 1635, and arrived in Boston on June 7th. That was sixty-six days at sea on a ship that was perhaps 80 feet long and 24 feet at its widest point, with two decks of occupancy for the entire length of the vessel. In that extended time and limited space people got to know each other very well, probably better than they ever wanted.

They very likely landed in Boston, the main port of entry at the time. Boston was founded in 1630, and within five or six years Michael

Leppingwell and Thomas were there. At the time of their arrival Boston had a population of several hundred people, less than one thousand. This was the very beginning of New England, and they were among the earliest immigrants. Michael probably found work as a tanner, the craft he is known to have practiced in the nearby town of Woburn a few years later. Thomas, it would be reasonable to assume, would have been his assistant in the tanning work, helping to turn animal hides into leather.

Thomas Leffingwell did not stay with Michael for long. In a very short time, probably within a year or perhaps two, Thomas struck out on his own into the world. Why he did so is not known. Hopefully, it was done for positive reasons and on a friendly basis. There are other possibilities, though. Perhaps Michael was a troubled person who wrongly cast out or forced out his younger brother, or was a harsh and insufferable authoritarian who could no longer be tolerated by Thomas. Maybe it was the other way around, with Thomas being a headstrong youth who could not be governed, so was either thrown out or ran away on his own accord. His later life would not demonstrate such personal characteristics, but perhaps he matured. Just a boy of twelve or thirteen years of age, Thomas was in the position of contemplating that he was very far from England now, and was going alone into the daunting wilderness of the New World to make his way in life.

As has been seen, in 1637 Thomas Leffingwell appeared in the sparsely populated forests of Connecticut, in the company of Uncas, the chief (or sachem) of the Mohegans. How did he get into that situation? It seems unlikely that a youth simply walked into the forests alone to see what would happen. The woods were a dangerous place where an inexperienced boy could easily get killed by man, beast, or weather.

Two scenarios seem to have possibly occurred. Because Michael Leppingwell was a tanner, Thomas probably knew hunters and trappers who had brought hides to Michael. Thomas may have gone with them into the forests, learning their trades, and working his way down about a hundred miles to the coast of Connecticut. Being a tanner, trapper, and hunter would have afforded Thomas Leppingwell, now going by the name Leffingwell, the opportunity and time to be with Uncas and the Mohegans. The area of Connecticut "abounded with beaver" and in the 1620s the fur trade reached 10,000 beaver skins annually. Indians would exchange beaver skins for European trade goods previously unknown to them. Wampum, consisting of coastal clam shells made into a necklace of beads or into a belt, became used as intercultural money.[14] These facts reasonably inspire the thought that Thomas Leffingwell was a young trapper and hunter in the forests, in the company of Englishmen teaching him the way of the woods, mingling with the Indians in the beaver trade.

There is an alternative explanation which is speculative but reasonably possible. Leffingwell may have volunteered in Massachusetts to be a soldier in the Pequot War, and then been sent to Fort Saybrook, Connecticut. There he would have been part of a military operation in which Uncas and the Mohegans fought on the side of the English against other Indian tribes. Either of these alternatives could have given Thomas Leffingwell the opportunity and time to be among the Indians and to come into contact with Uncas. Again, in the absence of definite information, Leffingwell's going to Connecticut could have happened in yet another unknown way.

Arriving in 1637, it is no exaggeration to say that Thomas Leffingwell was present at the creation of Connecticut. The area was named for the river the Indians called "Quonehtacut," meaning, "the long river." For centuries the land had been inhabited by various Native American tribes, the population of which had very recently been decimated by diseases unintentionally brought by the English. The Pequots and Mohegans and nearby tribes had lost as much as 80% of their population. It was a devastating loss. Meanwhile, English settlers from Massachusetts began establishing small towns in Windsor in 1633, Wethersfield in 1634, and Hartford in 1636. The fort at Saybrook was established in 1635.

The great sachem Uncas was born in the Pequot tribe, and wanted to become its chief. When his rival Sassacus was chosen instead, the young and dissatisfied Uncas broke away from the Pequots and with his followers formed a new tribe, the Mohegans.[15] It was thereafter his goal to depose Sassacus and punish the Pequots. Uncas was a strong, politically savvy, skillful and violent man, yet would sometimes demonstrate a grateful and generous heart. He could see that time, weapons, and numbers were on the side of the English, and that there was no future in fighting them. The wiser course was to be on the winning side, working *with* the English instead of against them. So he sought a path of cooperation with the English rather than conflict. For many years Uncas was the preeminent Native American leader in eastern Connecticut.

When Thomas Leffingwell met Uncas, the people of Connecticut were in the middle of the Pequot War. Whether he went there as a trapper or as a soldier, being with Uncas at that time leads to the inevitable conclusion that Leffingwell himself became caught up in that war. He could not have been there in 1637, with Uncas, and not been a part of it. The English war against the Pequots was ruthless, almost one of extermination for that entire tribe. It is not possible now to know what his involvement in the war was other than to say he was there. It must have been a shock to young Leffingwell to experience the war and witness its cruelty and violence. He may have been present at the massacre of the Pequots at Mystic River on May 26, 1637.

A depiction of the Pequot War by Charles S. Reinhart. (Lion Gardiner, a Tale of the Pequot War, by Isabella H. Graham, 1918.)

Living Among the Mohegans

Perhaps the best way to understand Leffingwell's association with the Native Americans is to start with the known facts, and then deduce from them what actions it took for them to have been true. This requires getting out ahead of the story chronologically, but gives a better view of the nature of his relationship with the Indians. These facts will be individually discussed in context and in more detail later in this book.

Leffingwell said, and the record of his life shows, that he was a friend of Uncas and the Mohegans, so he did things that were consistent with that fact. He took the actions, and was in the places, which were necessary for that to have occurred. He therefore had to have spent much time in the Indian camps, and with the Indians in general, and with Uncas in particular.

A situation was reported years later in which someone mentioned in passing that Leffingwell was crossing the Connecticut River in the company of three Indians. This demonstrated his ongoing friendly relationship with the Mohegans, and his ease of casual association with them.

Years later Leffingwell acted as a court interpreter for the Indian leaders, so it is known that he spoke the Algonquian language of the Mohegans.[16] This single fact tells a great deal about him. Languages are not learned in a day. That he could speak in their tongue necessarily reveals that he spent a great deal of time with them, learning to understand word by word what they were saying, and learning to communicate with them himself. The time that he was among them he was likely in their villages and camps. It is easy to picture in the mind a teenage youth, dressed in the clothing of the day, speaking English with his own Essex accent of Old England, mixing with the Native Americans in a friendly environment. In this manner he learned through time and by experience the Mohegan language and way of life.

In a later war between tribes, when Uncas and his warriors were besieged by the Narragansetts and in danger of starvation and death, the Indian sachem sent word to his good friend Leffingwell, who then risked his own life to save them. That Leffingwell would take a chance on possible death to help Uncas speaks volumes about both his character as well as his concern for the chief and his people. Clearly he cared about them because he knew them well and lived a life that brought him into regular contact with them. Uncas, in gratitude to his friend, gave land to Leffingwell.

Still later, Leffingwell's property in Norwich was the place where Mohegans pitched their wigwams and stayed to defend the English settlers against hostile Indian tribes. Being on his farm put the Native Americans into the daily lives of Leffingwell and his family. The relationship had to have been positive for him to have allowed this, and to have continued it over the years. It bespeaks an affection for the Mohegan people. Thomas's grandson Samuel Leffingwell 2d testified that he was well acquainted with the sons and grandsons of Uncas, indicating an inter-family familiarity.[17] Samuel knew these Indians because his grandfather who raised him knew Uncas

9

and his family.

Much later, while on a royal commission to look into the Mohegan land claims made by Uncas, Leffingwell sought to permanently preserve to the Mohegan people the homeland where the tribe had lived. His actions and decisions over a lifetime showed a genuine respect for the Mohegan people, and he lived a life and had the character that made this possible.

All of these facts show that the description of young Thomas Leffingwell by Dr. Leffingwwell as being in the forests with Uncas and the Mohegans, living in their villages and acquiring their language, was a sound one. Leffingwell had a lifetime of good relationships with Uncas and the Mohegans, and really all men, throughout his life. He was loyal to the friends he made among the Native Americans, and they were loyal to him. He lived the life and did the things that made all these facts true, and in considering them, one can catch a glimpse of the actual man, Thomas Leffingwell.

Returning to the story in 1637, Thomas Leffingwell arrived in Connecticut as a young teenager and had fallen into the company of Uncas and the Mohegans. It should be noted that he was not the only English friend of the sachem, nor was he the most important. Captain John Mason beyond all doubt was the most prominent and best English friend of Uncas. Mason was the commander of all English forces in the Pequot War and a well known and faithful supporter of the chief during and after the war, and for all of Mason's life. Leffingwell did not have the prominence or military rank to match Mason, but was nonetheless a genuine friend and supporter of Uncas, one appreciated by the sachem himself. Other Englishmen were good friends of Uncas, as well; it was something the chief intentionally fostered as a matter of both personality and of political policy.

Mason was the commander at Fort Saybrook and of all the English forces in the war, both those from Connecticut and those from Massachusetts who were sent to Connecticut to help. He commanded all European men in the area, including both soldiers and civilians, and this wide net swept in Thomas Leffingwell, whether trapper or soldier. Although his rank was the equivalent of a military general, Mason has gone into history as a Captain. The soldiers he commanded were not English regulars as we think of redcoats in the Revolutionary War, but rather men (and boys like Leffingwell) recruited from the local people already in New England.

It may have been that in the late 1630s and 1640s Captain Mason took the young Leffingwell under his wing, and watched out for his interests, helping him move from soldiering or trapping to farming, and from a socially marginal teenage boy to a man of substance owning land. There are scattered facts to suggest this possibility. Because he was already picking up the Mohegan language, it could have been that Captain Mason selected Leffingwell as an aide and used the boy as a translator with Uncas and his warriors. After the war Mason advocated giving land to the soldiers who had served, and Leffingwell ended up owning land in Saybrook directly adjacent to Mason, perhaps indicating that Mason himself arranged that land for Thomas. Years later, when there was the migration of many residents from Saybrook to the new town of Norwich, Mason and Leffingwell were among them, and they lived as neighbors in this new town until Mason's death in 1672.

After the war ended in 1638, Leffingwell stayed on in the vicinity of Fort Saybrook. He was still only about fourteen years old. It seems likely that he would have been a soldier at Fort Saybrook, transitioning over the years from a soldier in the fort to a planter just outside of it. Between 1638 and 1647 Thomas Leffingwell went from being an unattached youth with no family to being a husband, father, and landowner in Saybrook. Perhaps, as has been seen, the transformation happened with a considerable boost from Captain Mason.

Life in Saybrook after the war was peaceful. The ruthless conquest and near extermination of the Pequots struck terror into the hearts of all the Indians in New England, and they made no open war upon the English for nearly forty years. Yet there was no peace between and among the various Indian tribes. Uncas and the Mohegans were in a constant struggle with the neighboring tribes in a rough and often deadly competition. While the English farmers were peacefully planting crops and going to church in their isolated settlements, in the nearby woods the Native Americans were cutting each other's throats.

With the countryside in a violent turmoil, it was required that every man also be a soldier, ready for a call to arms at every moment. Writing in the 1790s, historian Benjamin Trumbull said that in the 1630s each English town was "required to take care that the inhabitants were well furnished with arms and ammunition, and kept in a constant state of defence. As these infant settlements were filled and surrounded with numerous savages, the people conceived themselves in danger when they lay down and when they rose up, when they went out and when they came in. Their circumstances were such, that it was judged necessary for every man to be a soldier."[18] Though the urgency slowly eased over the years, it was renewed again before and during the King Phillip's War in the 1670s. This was how Leffingwell lived day to day for many years of his life - on the alert, ready to respond as necessary.

One day, amidst the Native American in-fighting, a plea for help actually did come to him. Chief Uncas was in trouble. The response of Thomas Leffingwell put him into the history books.

Chapter 2

The Rescue of Chief Uncas and the Mohegans

After helping the English to victory in the Pequot War, the power and prestige of Uncas among the both the settlers and the tribes of eastern Connecticut was at an all time high. That peak began to erode, however. In 1643, with the complicity of Uncas, his brother Wawequa killed the Narragansett chief Miantonomoh. While both tribes maintained peace with the English, the Mohegans and Narragansetts descended into years of revenge wars against each other.

This situation led to the most famous incident in the life of Thomas Leffingwell. In considering the accounts of what happened, it is wise to remember a caution given in a speech at the Norwich Jubilee in 1859 on the 200th anniversary of the founding of the town. "These stirring incidents which tradition perpetuates should be reviewed by the muse of romance, rather than of history," said Daniel C. Gilman. "It is probable that we have the facts in outline, though we have the outlines only."[19] The facts that are available come from four brief statements by Thomas Leffingwell himself in 1667, by descendant William Leffingwell in 1796 and used in Benjamin Trumbull's history of Connecticut, by Norwich town historian Frances Manwaring Caulkins in the 1860s, and a family oral tradition by descendant John Leffingwell in 1905. These latter three were written 150 to 250 years after the event, and are therefore subject to caution.

At one point in these inter-tribal wars, Uncas and his people, greatly reduced in numbers, became surrounded by the more numerous Narragansetts, and were on the verge of being starved into submission or death. Uncas and his dwindling band of followers were trapped at what is called Fort Shantok in the heart of the Mohegan homeland. With such armaments as the Narragansetts had, the position was practically impregnable, and they had no way of reducing it except by siege and starving its occupants into surrender.

"During the wars between Uncas and the Narragansets," Benjamin Trumbull wrote in the 1790s, the Narragansetts under Chief Pessicus "besieged his fort, near the bank of the Thames [then called the Pequot River], until his provisions were nearly exhausted, and he found that he, and his men, must soon perish, by famine or sword, unless he could obtain speedy relief."[20]

The Mohegans, desperate for help, turned to their allies from the Pequot War. They had helped the English settlers in time of war, and now they hoped their friends would return the favor and help them. "Uncas, their sachem," wrote descendant William Leffingwell, "found means to inform the settlers at Saybrook of their distress, and the danger they [the English] would be in from the Narragansetts if the Mohegans tribe were cut off."[21] It was indeed in the English interest to save the chief and his people.

It seems most probable that an Indian messenger came by canoe to Fort Saybrook, landing on the shore adjacent to the fortifications. This was the land owned by Thomas Leffingwell. He was already a friend of Uncas and his people, a speaker of their language, and it may be that the Mohegan warrior was sent directly to him. Though its accuracy is questionable due to several obvious errors, a short version of the story apparently handed down through the Leffingwell family and published by John Leffingwell in 1905 says that the message was in fact sent specifically to Thomas Leffingwell.[22]

However it came, whether by intention or by happenstance, the plea of Uncas for immediate assistance ended up in the hands of Thomas Leffingwell. In just what capacity he was acting at that moment, whether soldier, planter, friend, or all three, is not known. It was stated in Trumbull's history that Leffingwell had the rank of "ensign," but he did not acquire that rank until years later. What is important is that Leffingwell did not simply pass the request for help along to others to deal with. He took the plea personally and took action himself in response to it. Applying a literary phrase that would be written later, this was Thomas Leffingwell's "crowded hour."[a]

The message from Uncas was that he and his people needed help, especially food, immediately. The historian Trumbull states that "upon this intelligence, one Thomas Leffingwell, an ensign at Saybrook, an enterprising, bold man, loaded a canoe with beef, corn, and pease."[23] Not

---

[a] "The instant I received the order I sprang on my horse and then my 'crowded hour' began," wrote Theodore Roosevelt (1858-1919) about the charge up San Juan Hill in the Spanish-American War. "One crowded hour of glorious life is worth an age without a name." Thomas Osbert Mordaunt (1730-1809).

only did Leffingwell act at once and on his own initiative, but with his own food resources, emptying his own supply in the house by the river for the benefit of the Mohegans.

It seems a certainty that the Mohegan warrior who brought the message went back with Leffingwell to Uncas, using his knowledge of the enemy positions to help guide the rescuer by night through the hostile lines of the Narragansetts to the Mohegans. It is inconceivable that a warrior would bring dire news from Uncas that immediate help is drastically needed, then himself go on a break while Leffingwell saved the Mohegans. No Native American would have wanted to face Uncas with that conduct. So it is reasonable to believe that Leffingwell went with the assistance of at least one Mohegan, and the 1905 account given by John Leffingwell says there were three.

It is most fortunate that we have a statement from Thomas Leffingwell himself, written several years later, that directly mentions this event. The statement is given in full here, with the portion about the rescue of Uncas in italics. Other aspects of this letter will be considered later.

To the Right Worshipful Court assembled at Hartford:

Whereas you are by God and his people constituted a court of Justice and have approved yourselves in matters of Justice: *I am encouraged to recommend to your considerations a case depending between Uncas the Moheagen Sachem and myself. It is not unknown to him and others what damage in my outward estate I have suffered by his men; and yet notwithstanding when he and his people were famishing being besieged by many enemies I did afford him provision for their relief, although it was to the hazard of all my outward comforts, the enemy knowing what supply I had and did afford him.* Upon these and such like reasons Uncas hath several times offered me some land for my recompense and just satisfaction and hath expressed the same to the Major who is acquainted with the truth of these things, but order requireth me to propound the matter to your worshipful considerations desiring your approbation of the way Uncas hath propounded for my satisfaction. Its far from me to desire land in such place where my possessing of it might hinder a plantation [i.e., town] work, or any such public good, but providence presenting such an equal means for the relief of my family by inclining the heart of a heathen to observe rules of justice and with gratitude for that which he hath received and this coming on without any importunity on my part I hope your worships will not judge me guilty of inordinate seeking after that which I ought not but I would not be negligent in improving the present hint of providence. So hoping you will not reject the proposition made, but show your worshipful approbation for the most real affecting of it and I cease giving you any further trouble. I remain your humble servant.

Norwich, May the 6, 1667. Thomas Leffingwell.[24]

This letter says a lot about Thomas Leffingwell. It is well composed, indicating an easy literacy, and leading one to believe that he received an education as a youth in England for there was no such opportunity once he arrived in America. Leffingwell stated that he risked "all of my outward comforts" to save the Mohegans. He also risked his life, as the inter-tribal Indian wars were violent and deadly. He could expect to be killed if caught in this rescue effort. Thomas Leffingwell was either a fearless man, or a courageous one who suppressed his fear and took action. As the historian Trumbull truly said, he was "an enterprising, bold man."

The type of canoe used by Leffingwell is not known. It is possible that he used a canoe, or canoes, operable by one man, and that he loaded his own canoe and that of his Native messenger(s) with food supplies. It seems likely, however, that he would have used the largest canoe available, perhaps one up to forty feet in length, operated by two men (Leffingwell and the messenger). Such a canoe could carry a considerable amount of cargo, sufficient to feed many people back at the Mohegan fort. Smaller canoes were not well suited for going into the currents and waves of Long Island Sound, which is part of the Atlantic Ocean. There a larger canoe would be more serviceable and steady.

Leffingwell and his Indian messenger(s) headed out into the waters of the Connecticut River. This was no small trip. They had to go a mile to reach the east bank of the Connecticut River where it met the ocean. At the mouth of the river they turned left into Long Island Sound and headed east for about thirteen miles through the waves along the Atlantic coast. They turned left again into the Pequot (Thames) River, going north upriver for another thirteen miles. This all took time. The journey would have taken a great deal of physical strength and continual strenuous exertion. According to William Leffingwell's account in 1796, the rescuers "in the night time paddled from Saybrook into the Thames" River.[25]

The approximate route of Thomas Leffingwell going from Saybrook on the Connecticut River, into Long Island Sound, and up the Pequot (Thames) River to Fort Shantok, is marked on this 1766 map of Connecticut. (Library of Congress.)

Meanwhile, the waiting Uncas was restless. "A fanciful legend has in later times been connected with this adventure," wrote historian Frances Caulkins two hundred years later. "It would be difficult now [the 1860s] to ascertain what degree of truth belongs to it. It is said that the expected relief from Saybrook was delayed much longer than the hungry and impatient Mohegans had anticipated ; and that each night Uncas left the fort and crept along the bank of the river, skulking by the water's edge, till he came to a rocky and precipitous point, which juts into the stream, a little above Massapeag Cove. Here, under shelter of the rock, the sachem remained till nearly day-light, with his sleepless eyes upon the river, and his ear intent to catch the slightest sound of a falling oar, and it was not till the second or third night of his watch that Leffingwell arrived. The ledge of rock on which the sachem sat in his midnight watch has since obtained the name of *Uncas' Chair*."[26]

At last, Leffingwell and his supplies arrived in the darkness. Having known Uncas for several years, and having been with his tribe long enough to learn their language, Leffingwell had undoubtedly spent a great deal of time at this area and was well familiar with the place where Uncas was trapped. The warrior with him would have known the details of where both friend and foe were specifically located. They had to be very careful, and absolutely silent. Any detection by the Narragansetts could mean immediate death, or worse, a slow tortured death. "Under cover of the night," historian Trumbull wrote of Leffingwell, he "paddled... into the Thames, and had the address [the 1790s meaning of 'address" included 'skill, dexterity, skillful management;' Webster's Dictionary 1828] to get the whole into the fort."[27] Tradition says that Leffingwell met Uncas at the "chair of Uncas." It was surely a momentous and emotional occasion as the two men came together at this perilous time, their friendship forever strengthened.

Caulkins continued her description of the incident as known in the 1860s. "No sooner was this timely supply of provisions safely lodged in the fortress, than loud shouts of exultation were uttered by the besieged, to the astonishment of the Narragansetts, who were unable to divine the cause of this midnight triumph" she wrote. "At the dawn of day, however, the secret was disclosed; the Mohegans elevated a large piece of beef on a pole, and thus gave notice of the relief they had obtained. The Narragansetts dared not assail either the persons or property of the English, but we can readily believe that they beheld the boat lying by the shore with bitter feelings of exasperation, and poured out a torrent of threats and invectives against its officious owners. That they saw Leffingwell, and knew it was he that brought the supplies, is evident from Leffingwell's own testimony.... Finding that there was no chance of reducing the Mohegans while they were thus supported, the Narragansetts abandoned the siege and returned home."[28]

The number of Mohegan warriors, women and children trapped at Fort Shantok is not known. It was few enough that they could be trapped, but numerous enough that they could not be overwhelmed by their enemies. The provisions brought by Leffingwell were sufficient in size and nature to convince the Narragansetts that continuing the siege was hopeless.

Leffingwell had saved Uncas as well as the Mohegan people. The broader English community then stepped in to help and protect Uncas and his people by stationing soldiers to defend the Mohegan lands. The Narragansetts, who did not want war with the English, accepted peace for a time. The moment of immediate danger to the Mohegans had passed.

It is difficult to overstate the importance of what Thomas Leffingwell did. Without his rescue, what would have been the outcome of these events? Uncas would most certainly have been killed. Ultimately, the besieged Mohegans would have surrendered to the Narragansetts, and Uncas would have been executed just like the Narragansett chief Miantonomoh had been executed by the Mohegans. With their chief dead, the Mohegans would have been scattered and possibly absorbed by another tribe. The firm ally of the English would have been lost, then and for the future King Philip's War. The conveyance of the deed from Uncas to the settlers of Norwich would not have happened when and as it did, and the history of that town would have been altered. In the coming years the friendly services of the Mohegans to the English would not have happened. In short, history would have unfolded very differently.

Uncas knew the danger that he had been in, and that he would have been killed. He was forever grateful to Thomas Leffingwell for saving his life and his leadership of the tribe. Their friendship was cemented, and their bond would never be broken. The Mohegan sachem would be generous in giving him land, and the Englishman would always work to protect the remaining tribal lands. "Upon these and such like reasons Uncas hath several times offered me some land for my recompense and just satisfaction," Leffingwell wrote later of the chief's response to the rescue.[29]

There exists today on the Mohegan Reservation a marble monument of appreciation to Thomas Leffingwell, commemorating his actions of long ago. The monument was created in November 1898 by the Connecticut Society of the Colonial Dames of America, but it is allowed and maintained now by the Mohegan Tribe. It is a cone-shaped formation of stones shaped like a wigwam, with a plaque that reads: "Here was the Fort of Uncas, Chief of the Mohegans and Friend of the English. Here, in 1645, when besieged by the Narragansetts, he was relieved by the bravery of Lieutenant Thomas Leffingwell." The monument was originally located on the west side of the Pequot (Thames) River, four miles from Norwich, to mark the spot known as the "chair of Uncas."[30] Later, it was moved to its current location at the Mohegan Cemetery.

There are lingering questions about Thomas Leffingwell's rescue of Uncas and the Mohegans. Did he act alone, or were other Enlishmen with him? Just when did this event happen? Did Uncas deed the land that later included all or most of Norwich to Leffingwell in appreciation for his actions? Was Thomas Leffingwell the real life role model for the fictional character Hawkeye in The Last of the Mohegans?

Did Leffingwell Act Alone?

There are scattered statements in 19th and 20th century books and online on the Internet that deduce that other English settlers helped Leffingwell in rescuing Uncas. Beyond the four accounts mentioned above (Thomas Leffingwell himself 1667; descendants William Leffingwell 1796 used by Benjamin Trumbull, and John Leffingwell 1905; and Norwich historian Frances Caulkins 1860s), several versions of the story have been written, based upon no additional facts, but some of which state the suppositions and deductions of the authors interwoven into them as though they were known facts. They simply state that other people besides Leffingwell were involved. Various people are even named, including Thomas Tracy, William Hyde, Thomas Miner/Minor, John Mason, and even the Saybrook pastor, James Fitch.

Perhaps abstract logic suggests others *must* have been involved. How can one canoe full of food supplies, even a forty foot one, relieve the starving Mohegan people? How many Mohegans were trapped there? Why would Leffingwell act alone? It may have been these questions that caused historian John W. DeForest to write in 1852 that, "It is probable, *although not certain*, that Leffingwell was accompanied in his expedition by two other men named Thomas Tracy and Thomas Miner."[31] [Emphasis added.] DeForest fails to cite any sources for adding these names, apparently stating his own figuring of the event. Perhaps on the basis of the DeForest book, even the Mohegan Tribe online website[32] states that Tracy and Miner were in on the rescue, though they cite only to Caulkins in *History of Norwich* (who never says anyone else was involved). Other 1800s books, and some genealogical works, name others as being present.

The best case for another person's presence is for Thomas Tracy. When Leffingwell was rewarded by Uncas in 1667 with a gift of land for saving the Mohegan people, Thomas Tracy was a co-grantee of the 400 acres (which was to be divided between the two Englishmen). From this fact the idea originated that Tracy had been a partner with Leffingwell in the relief of Uncas. When Leffingwell wrote his letter to the colonial legislature, he did not say that Tracy had been there, and, as has been quoted, Tracy and all others were excluded by Leffingwell's use of the word "I." There is no record that Tracy objected to this phraseology at the time. Uncas could have given the land jointly to two men but for different reasons. Referring to the conclusion that the joint deed shows Tracy was with Leffingwell in the Fort Shantok rescue, local historian Caulkins rejected the proposition in the 1860s. "But the inference is not necessary," she wrote. "Tracy was much employed in public affairs, and might obtain the grant in recompense for other services."[33] Some descendants of Tracy reject that conclusion, asserting that up to that time Tracy had not been involved in public service.

The Thomas Leffingwell monument at the Mohegan Reservation is in the shape of wigwam.

"Here stood the fort of Uncas, Sachem of the Mohegans and Friend of the English. Here in 1645 when besieged by the Narragansetts he was relieved by the bravery of Lieut. Thomas Leffingwell."

"Erected by the Connecticut Society of Colonial Dames. 1898."

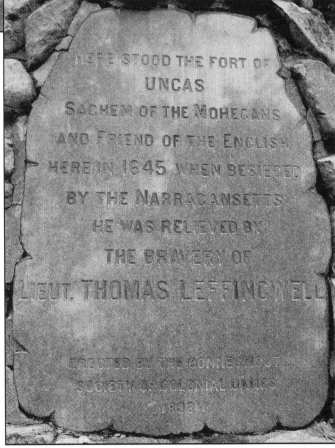

Of course, what actually happened and who participated was known at the time to Leffingwell, Uncas, the Mohegans, and many others. The consideration here is only attempting to examine what evidence there is for the involvement of other Englishmen. It appears that there is no historical record upon which to add the presence of other settlers or soldiers. Leffingwell himself, the man who did the deed and who beyond all doubt was present, in 1667 said (repeating the earlier quotation but with an emphasis on certain phrasing):

> ... I am encouraged to recommend to your considerations a case depending between Uncas the Moheagen Sachem and myself... [W]hen he and his people were famishing being besieged by many enemies *I did afford him provision* for their relief, although it was to the hazard of all *my* outward comforts, the enemy knowing *what supply I had* and did afford him. Upon these and such like reasons Uncas hath several times offered *me* some land for my recompense and just satisfaction...

Thomas Leffingwell, Norwich, May the 6, 1667.[34]

This statement certainly implies that no other Englishmen were involved. Leffingwell quite clearly says that "when he and his people were famishing being besieged by many enemies **I** did afford him provision for their relief" from "what supply **I** had." This word "I" is beyond all doubt a singular word, exclusive of other people. Based upon his life and character, there is no basis to believe that Leffingwell would have claimed exclusive credit for this event where it was not his due, or would have denied credit to people who were his friends, especially when they were still alive to contradict any mis-statement of truth he would make in the public record. Also, he says the "the case was one depending between Uncas and **myself**," Uncas "offered **me** some land for **my** recompense." These are quite clearly singular words, and do not reference any other party, such as in "offered *us* some land." Furthermore, the phrase "the enemy knowing what supply I had and did afford him" very much indicates that Leffingwell was a man known to the Narragansetts, that they would afterward know that it was specifically him who had supplied Uncas, and they would know where to find him as an individual to exact revenge. He did not have the psychological advantage of strength in numbers, of being only one of a number of people who helped.

Frances Caulkins wrote in her history of Norwich that "no later investigations either enlarge or vary the account given by the venerable historian of Connecticut [Trumbull]."[35] This is still true. Speaking for himself and his co-author of *The Leffingwell Record*, Dr. Albert Leffingwell wrote that,"We, therefore, claim for Thomas Leffingwell the honor of having dared and done the deed alone...[36]

Like so many other aspects of Thomas Leffingwell's early life, the full truth is not known. Only the outlines of facts are available after these four centuries. History is always subject to being overturned by the later discovery of old evidence hidden away somewhere, but it appears that Leffingwell was the only Englishman involved in the rescue.

What Year Did Leffingwell Rescue Uncas?

An interesting footnote to this famous episode is that it not known exactly when it happened. The historian Trumbull assigned no date to the event. The lack of a newspaper or other contemporaneous written records has left the timing uncertain. The date attributed to the siege is generally stated as 1645,[37] but others date it as late as 1656[38] or 1657.[39] The Mohegan wars with their Indian neighbors dragged on during all of the intervening years.

Frances Caulkins says the 1657 date cannot be sustained because it was mixing up the Fort Shantok event with another round of tribal struggles that year. "It might be the safest course to leave the period of this incident indefinite, but there is sufficient historic evidence to justify us in assigning it definitely to May or June 1645...."[40]

However, her claim for 1645 does not seem sustainable when examining the life of Thomas Leffingwell. He said that he gave assistance from his own provisions, which would require him at that time to have been a man of substance and supplies. In 1645 Leffingwell was only twenty-one years old and single, probably not an owner of land, and unlikely to have an abundance of his own supplies. By the 1650s, however, he was older and a landowner of means. This seems to support a later date.

As with so many things, the full truth of the matter is lost in time.

Did Uncas Give the Whole Area
of Norwich to Thomas Leffingwell?

The historian Trumbull said that "for this service, Uncas gave said Leffingwell a deed of a great part, if not of the whole town of Norwich." This did not happen and was simply a historian's mistake. There never was such a deed, and no such document was ever mentioned by Leffingwell or anyone else, nor was one ever recorded in official records or preserved in any way. Trumbull was confused on this point because descendant William Leffingwell, his source of information, made an ambiguous statement.

After rescuing the Mohegans, William Leffingwell wrote 150 years later that Thomas Leffingwell "received a deed from Uncas of the town of Norwich." It was a cryptic statement that was conflated beyond reality. That unfortunately phrased statement was true, but that particular deed was to more than thirty men, one of whom was Thomas Leffingwell. "In June 1659," Trumbull wrote, "Uncas, with his two sons, Owaneco and Attawanhood, by a more formal and authentic deed, made over unto said Leffingwell, John Mason, Esq. the Rev. James Fitch, and others, consisting of thirty-five proprietors, the whole township of Norwich, which is about nine miles square. The company, at this time, gave Uncas and his sons about seventy pounds, as a further compensation for so large and fine a tract."[41] That deed was signed and approved by the colonial government.

Beyond that deed, it is definitely known that Leffingwell was given a half interest in 400 acres as his reward for rescuing Uncas. That land was not in Norwich. Trumbull, or William Leffingwell who gave him the information, confused the two documents.

Writing history is a hazardous undertaking. Finding and learning every fact and putting each one in context and chronology, while sorting out false traditions and long ago rumors, is impossible. That was true for Trumbull in the 1790s, and it is true now for this book. Trumbull knew this occupational hazard, and his occasional error should be forgiven. Leffingwell never claimed the right of any such deed. It simply never happened.

Was Thomas Leffingwell the Inspiration for Hawkeye?

Dr. Albert Leffingwell in *The Leffingwell Record* suggested that Thomas Leffingwell was "the prototype, perhaps" of the fictional character variously called "Natty Bumppo" and "Hawkeye" in the books by James Fenimore Cooper.[42] This is a fascinating thought. Was the character Hawkeye in the fictional book *The Last of the Mohicans* based on the real life man Thomas Leffingwell?

The starting point of this analysis should begin with the fact that the author

Cooper took real names, people and events, mixed them around with a fictional story line and characters, and came up with interesting historical fiction. In his lifetime he wrote five books collectively known as The Leatherstocking Tales, which were fictional accounts of strong men in perilous situations in New York during the French and Indian War.

Cooper's well of historical information goes deep into Connecticut, where he went to Yale College in the first decade of the 1800s. He was an observant young man, very much interested in the Connecticut frontier and its people and history.

Cooper took facts and imagination and rearranged them into something new - fictional and yet familiar. He called the Mohegans the Mohicans. The Connecticut frontier of the 1630s became New York in the 1750s. The sadly dwindling number of the Mohegans over the years suggested to that author the concept of the Mohicans being down to their very last man. One of the central figures in the book was Uncas, the son of Chingachgook, whose name obviously came from the actual chief Uncas. *The Last of the Mohicans* story has Hawkeye at one point escaping capture by the enemy by jumping off a waterfall, which was undoubtedly suggested by the legend of the rival Narragansett chief Miantonomoh jumping over a waterfall to escape Uncas, who jumped after him. The character Magua, the evil Indian of the book, is likely a simple co-opting of the tribal name of Maqua.

It is obvious, then, that Cooper knew early Connecticut history, and used it in forming his fictional stories. He surely knew the tale of how the real Uncas and his men were trapped and surrounded in a deadly siege by their Indian enemies, and that he sent for help to his allies, the English. That request for assistance came to Thomas Leffingwell, an Englishman who was a true friend of the Indians who spoke their language and had lived with them. He loaded a canoe with foodstuffs and paddled through the night, evading the enemy and bringing relief to Uncas. It cannot be proven but it is most likely true that James Fenimore Cooper knew specifically about Thomas Leffingwell.

In rescuing Uncas, Leffingwell presents a white man, a friend of the Indians, speaking their language and familiar with their customs, intrepid and daring in saving his friends, strong and skilled with a canoe, familiar with the woods and the rivers, and tireless and fearless when faced with danger. These personal qualities bring into view Cooper's character Hawkeye, a man of those same virtues. In this manner, we have the reasonable suggestion that Hawkeye is a personification of Leffingwell. It must be remembered, however, that Cooper never said that this was so. It is only a cautious inference.

In keeping this comparison in balance, however, it must be said that there were also dissimilarities between Leffingwell and Hawkeye. In *The Last of the Mohicans* Hawkeye often calls himself a "man without a cross," meaning that he is not a Christian, and who also rejects the beliefs of the Indians. Leffingwell, by contrast, was a devout New England Puritan in good standing. Hawkeye lived with the Indians in the forests, on the edge between Indian and English societies. Although Leffingwell started his New World life in the woods, he lived his life primarily as a prosperous farmer in the small colonial towns of Saybrook and Norwich. He married and had children in a settled community, and lived in a house and on a farm.

It is said that while James Fenimore Cooper was growing up in Cooperstown, New York, there was a woodsman with whom he had contact. His name was David Shipman, and his descendants say that he was the inspiration for Hawkeye. Shipman was born in Saybrook and had a history in the Mohegan country.

Cooper never said that any particular individual was the basis of Hawkeye/Natty Bumppo. The most that can fairly be said is that James Fenimore Cooper's fictional character Hawkeye was based on *the type of man* that Thomas Leffingwell was - a strong and brave white man, friend of Indians, friend of Uncas in particular, willing to do daring deeds, knowledgeable of the forests and rivers, and capable with a canoe.

It would be too much to say that Leffingwell was the sole inspiration for Hawkeye. In *The Last of the Mohicans*, Hawkeye was surely a composite character, possessing the qualities of several real men known to James Fenimore Cooper, as well as having those manly traits derived from Cooper's own fertile imagination.

Chapter 3

The Riddle of Wife Mary: English or Mohegan?

Upon his arrival in Connecticut Thomas Leffingwell was in a typical situation: he was young and single. Over half of the men in those early days arrived in their twenties and unmarried, and the lack of available brides pushed the average age at marriage up to thirty. The ratio of males to females decreased over the years until it was about even in the 1670s. One thing that eased the situation was that about a quarter of the male immigrants left soon after arrival, many going back to England.[43] Leffingwell beat those odds. He did not abandon his New World venture and move back to Britain, and he married well before age thirty.

Another of the mysteries we face in Thomas Leffingwell's life is a seemingly simple one: who was his wife? We know that it was a woman who was called Mary, that she stayed with him for more than sixty years, and that she was the mother of seven or more children. Beyond that, not much is known. There are radically different theories of who Mary was.

In the book *New England Marriages Prior to 1700* there is an entry for Thomas Leffingwell. It states that his wife's name is Mary, but is uncertain of the reliability of the last name of White, so the compiler put the name in brackets with a question mark next to it.[44] There is no underlying marriage record upon which this entry is based. The listing is simply the conclusion that Thomas and Mary, who were later known to be husband and wife, were married before 1648, the year of the birth of their first child, Rachel. They were probably married in 1647.

There are four possibilities of who Mary, the wife of Thomas Leffingwell really was. Each shall be considered, but in the end a definite conclusion cannot be reached. It is one of those areas of romance and mystery in his early life.

Mary White directly from England

"A tradition has obtained in some branches of the family," wrote Norwich historian Frances Manwaring Caulkins in the 1860s, "that when Thomas Leffingwell was twenty one years old he went back to England. He returned to Connecticut with a wife, Mary White, and his younger brother, Stephen,

27

leaving seven or eight other brothers in the old country." The only problem with this story is that there is not one shred of evidence to support it. There is no ship record showing that Leffingwell went back to England, although that absence may be unimportant because, as has been seen, there is no record that he came from England to the New World, though it is known for certain that he did. There is also no record of a Stephen Leffingwell in Connecticut. The story has a history of doubt, even in Caulkins' own mind. She wrote in a footnote that even then (the 1860s) she "was unable to decide whether these traditions should be ranked as fable or fact."[45]

Oral family history traditions are sometimes true. Thomas Leffingwell marrying Mary White on a trip to England, and bringing her to Connecticut, probably isn't.

Mary White from England through Massachusetts

A variation of this story could be that Mary White was born in England but was already in New England before she was married. From passenger lists its is known that there were at least two girls named Mary White who came to the New World in the 1630s. One, the daughter of John and Mary White, was on the ship *Lyon* in 1632. After four years in Massachusetts they moved on to Hartford, Connecticut. It is well documented that this Mary White married Jonathan Gilbert in Hartford on January 29, 1645. Clearly, she was not the wife of Thomas Leffingwell.

The other Mary White arrived on the ship *Abigail* in October 1635 with her parents, Edward and Martha White, and her older sister, Martha. She was eight years old according the ship's manifest, placing her birth year in 1627, or possibly late 1626. They came from the county of Kent in England and settled in Dorchester, Massachusetts, just south of Boston. Edward and Martha White appear to have both died many years later in Dorchester, and did not move to Connecticut. It is approximately a hundred miles from Dorchester to Saybrook, Connecticut, but it's feasible that Mary and Thomas Leffingwell somehow met. There were few English people in New England at that time, and Thomas had started in Massachusetts with his brother Michael, so their meeting is entirely possible.

Though not proven, there is some reason to believe that this girl may have eventually become the wife of Thomas Leffingwell. She was born in England, was available to be Leffingwell's wife, was in the right area, had the right name, and was the right age. No other facts can be found of her, such as a marriage to someone else, or a death or burial in another place. She may well be the one who became Mrs. Thomas Leffingwell.

There are a couple of elements of uncertainty, however. Mary White was a common name. There is no document connecting this Mary with Thomas Leffingwell. She could have married someone else without the record of the wedding surviving to the present, or perhaps she never married, or perhaps she died in her youth, though there is no record of that, either. She simply is available as a candidate for his wife because she exists in the historical record. Yet, undeniably, she is a good candidate to be the actual Mary Leffingwell.

Mary the daughter or sister of Uncas

There is an intriguing alternative explanation about Mary. Dr. Albert Leffingwell said that when he was a young man in the 1860s, his father told him that there was perhaps what was then considered to be a skeleton in the family history closet, that "according to an unwritten family tradition, the wife of our first ancestor was the sister or daughter of Uncas, the chief of the Mohegans." In preparing his book, the doctor learned from his distant cousin, Hiram Wheeler Leffingwell (1806-1897), that there was a similar report in his wing of the family. Albert was a descendant through Thomas and Mary Leffingwell's son, Thomas, while Hiram was descended through their son Nathaniel.[46] In 2009 a Leffingwell descendant posted a statement online asserting that older family members in her particular wing of the family had also stated that "there was an Indian in the family." The story, then, has been widespread within the far flung extended family.

Dr. Leffingwell said in 1897 that, going back in time, family history ends with Mary and could not be traced further. That appears to still be the case, unless Mary White of Dorchester, Massachusetts is used. Some modern day overly enthusiastic genealogists online have dubbed Mary as "Mary Uncas," or "Mary Singing Lark." These particular names are not based upon any verifiable historical fact, and should not be accepted unless and until there is actual proof.

It is known that English settlers did marry Indian women, and Uncas was known to marry out his daughters for political purposes of tribal alliances. One biographer of the sachem writes that "strategic marriage alliances provided Uncas with an additional tool for securing the allegiance of his new tributaries and establishing his legitimacy as a native community leader."[47] Uncas himself had married on just such a basis.

So perhaps this makes the proposition that Thomas Leffingwell's wife Mary was Native American within the realm of possibility.

There is an unverified story about Mary Leffingwell being the sister of a woman named Sarah Rood. (Her death, and the execution of her husband Thomas Rood, will be considered later in this book.) When Sarah Rood died she reportedly was buried in the Mohegan cemetery. This is offered as evidence that she was Mohegan, and that therefore her sister Mary was Mohegan as well. This point does not hold up to examination, however. The Rood property in Norwich, as well as others, overlapped onto the Mohegan cemetery, which became a point of sorrow to the tribe members in later years. When Sarah died, she was simply buried on her own property, which was on the Mohegan cemetery. It is not evidence that she was Mohegan.[48]

However, even if the Mohegan burial story is true, there is no convincing evidence that Sarah Rood was the sister of Mary Leffingwell. The book of New England pre-1700 marriages gave her no last maiden name,[49] and none has otherwise been found.

This supposed connection is based entirely upon the assertion that Thomas Leffingwell was the uncle of Thomas Rood's son, and therefore their wives must have been sisters. Another version is that Sarah was the sister of Thomas Leffingwell and that her name was Sarah Leffingwell Rood. This is pure fantasy. There is nothing whatever in the record to substantiate that he had a sister, or that, even if he did, she was in America, or that Sarah was that sister.

It seems most likely that Thomas Leffingwell's wife, Mary, was not a Mohegan. This is supported by several factors.

There are words written by Thomas Leffingwell himself that bear indirectly on the question of his wife's ancestry. Returning to his 1667 statement, it gives insight into how Leffingwell regarded Uncas. In the course of his statement, he says:

> To the Right Worshipful Court assembled at Hartford ;

> ... I am encouraged to recommend to your considerations a case depending between Uncas the Moheagen Sachem and myself. It is not unknown to him and others what damage in my outward estate I have suffered by his men; and yet notwithstanding when he and his people were

famishing being besieged by many enemies I did afford him provision for their relief, although it was to the hazard of all my outward comforts, the enemy knowing what supply I had and did afford him. Upon these and such like reasons Uncas hath several times offered me some land for my recompense and just satisfaction.... Its far from me to desire land in such place where my possessing of it might hinder a plantation [town] work... but providence presenting such an equal means for the relief of my family by inclining **the heart of a heathen** to observe rules of justice and with gratitude for that which he hath received.... I remain your humble servant,

Thomas Leffingwell. Norwich, May the 6, 1667.[50] [Emphasis added.]

There is absolutely nothing in this statement that indicates or even remotely hints that Uncas is the father of Thomas Leffingwell's wife, that Uncas is Leffingwell's father-in-law, that Uncas is the grandfather of Leffingwell's children, or that the two men are in any way related. There is nothing in the way of an implication that this is an inter-family conveyance of land. Rather, the description is completely in the language of an arm's length transaction. The land is simply a gift of gratitude by Uncas to Leffingwell, for things that Leffingwell had done for Uncas.

Furthermore, Leffingwell's statement about "the heart of a heathen" does not resound with any sort of familial affection or connection. It is a cold thing to say about the father or brother of one's wife, or about a co-grandfather of one's grandchildren. It does not ring true that Leffingwell would say Uncas had the "heart of a heathen" when his own wife was that man's daughter or sister, or when as a Mohegan she herself had once had the heart of a heathen. The Puritans did not kindly call people "heathen." The comment sounds instead like the 1600s baseline cultural divide between a white man and a Native American, and not something to be expected from a man whose wife was herself Indian and his children half Mohegan.

Another reason that it is unlikely that Mary was a Native American is that Thomas Leffingwell was in 1704 appointed to a Royal Commission charged with reviewing the legal status of Indian lands that Uncas had sought to be permanently preserved for the Mohegan people. (This will be discussed later in this book.) It seems unlikely that Leffingwell would have been appointed to such a position if he was Uncas's son-in-law or otherwise a kinsman of the plaintiff in a lawsuit. The commission's ultimate decision in favor of the Mohegans had vociferous critics, and one of their complaints would have certainly been that Commissioner Leffingwell was biased and unqualified because he was a relative of Uncas or married to a Mohegan wife. Yet those criticisms were not made at the time by opposing attorneys, and it is reasonable to presume that they were not made because those facts did not exist. Leffingwell was not married into the Uncas family or into the broader Mohegan tribe.

Dr. Albert Leffingwell points out another possibility of why some family members would have thought Mary was Mohegan. There were several Thomas Leffingwells over the generations after the one of whom we write here. It is possible that some other namesake married a Native American, and that a family truth was misapplied by later descendants to the first Thomas Leffingwell.

Dr. Leffingwell sums it up well about the story of Mary being a Mohegan. "At this day, it is of course impossible to say what amount of truth such tradition may possess," he wrote with emphasis added by this author, "and the reader is privileged - according to personal preferences - to accept or reject. We may say, perhaps, that while *the weight of probability is against it*, there is a chance that... there is a strain of Indian blood."[51] This assessment seems accurate. Mary Leffingwell probably was not Mohegan.

The fourth alternative for Mary

There remains yet another possibility of who the wife of Thomas Leffingwell really was. She could have been someone else entirely, a woman neither named White nor a relative of Uncas. She may have been a person of whom we know absolutely nothing except that she was called Mary Leffingwell in the historical record, and lived as his wife for more than sixty years.

Chapter 4

A Young Family Man in Saybrook

Following the Pequot War, Thomas Leffingwell became a very early settler of the community of Saybrook, near where the Connecticut River flows into the Atlantic Ocean. Two years earlier it had first been occupied by the English for the purpose of establishing a fortification. Saybrook was named for two of the English landowners who were granted the patent for the land where the town is located. They were "Lord Saye and Sele" and Lord Brooke, neither of whom ever made it across the ocean to Connecticut. Their titles, however, were combined to form the name Saybrook, originally spelled Saye-Brooke. Old maps often show the town as "Seabrook," which is a mistaken spelling even though it was still spoken as "Saybrook." In those days the word "sea" was pronounced "say," so "Seabrook" and "Saybrook" sounded the same.

Leffingwell was surely stationed there as a soldier during part of the Pequot War and afterward. By the late 1640s he had made the transition from a solitary youth on the frontier to an established citizen of the Saybrook community. "A settlement was soon made and named Saybrook," wrote historian Trumbull in the 1790s. He took notice that various men including "Thomas Leffingwell... were some of the principal planters."[52] This is a remarkable achievement for the young man. He came to Connecticut as a youth, alone, without wealth or family connections, and somehow elevated himself to a man of family, land and respected status.

Fort Saybrook was on the west bank of the Connecticut River, with a "North Cove" and a "South Cove" of the river above and below it. Thomas Leffingwell acquired land on the river directly north of the Saybrook fortification, where the water comes in to form the beginning of North Cove. It was described as "his house and home lot of two acres in the town, abutting North to the River, South to the Marsh, Southwest to the Land of Major Mason, Northwest to the Lands of Thomas Hanchat."[53] This property was easily accessible to that Mohegan messenger who brought a plea for help from Uncas. The land is depicted on the map below, and today is a very desirable waterfront property.

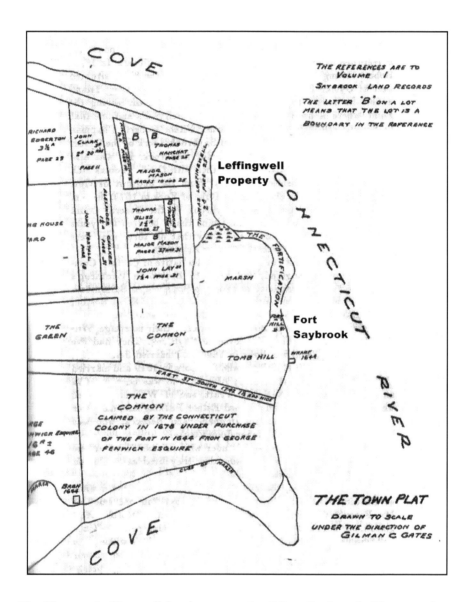

The Thomas Leffingwell land was north of Fort Saybrook. His waterfront property is shown in the photograph below, though his 1650s house was vastly more modest than any of the ones there now. (This 1935 map by Gilman C. Gates, to which the words "Leffingwell Property" and "Fort Saybrook" have been added, is in the public domain. Gates, Gilman C., Saybrook at the Mouth of the Connecticut, 1935, p. 153.)

The population in the 1600s was very low. As late as 1655 there were only about six thousand English settlers in all of Connecticut. Most men were farmers, and this included Thomas Leffingwell. He may have gone from trapper or soldier to farm laborer on someone else's land, then on to being a farmer on his own land. Bachelors rarely owned land,[54] so it was probably about 1647 that he obtained his own property. Although there is no supporting document to prove it as to Leffingwell specifically, he may have been granted land as payment for being a soldier in the Pequot War. On June 5, 1641, it was ordered by the Connecticut General Court "that Captain Mason shall... dispose of 500 more [acres] to such soldiers as joined with him in the service when they conquered the Indians there."[55] Leffingwell may well have been one of the beneficiaries of this grant.

In the frontier wilderness of Connecticut all men, including Thomas Leffingwell, were subject to being called on the be soldiers at any time. On June 2, 1647, in Saybrook it was "Ordered, that Captain Mason should for the peace, safety and good assurance of this Commonwealth, have the command of all soldiers and inhabitants of Seabrooke, and in case of alarum or danger by approach of an enemy, to draw forth or put the said soldiers and inhabitants in such posture for the defence of the place, as to him shall seem best."[56] In those days the enemy could be the Native Americans or the colonial rivals, the Dutch, or the French. Over the years, Thomas Leffingwell participated fully in the defense of his homeland. He was in the Pequot War, and he was an active member of the local militia. More than that, he worked for peace by his good relationships with the Mohegans in general, and with Uncas in particular.

A Congregational Church of Christ was formed ("gathered") in Saybrook in 1646 in the Great Hall of Fort Saybrook. Leffingwell would have been involved with this, in the least as a church member. The first pastor was 24-year-old James Fitch, who was only two years older than Leffingwell. A meetinghouse was soon built on Middle Lane. A beating drum would call the people to church services on the Sabbath. "The Saybrook meetinghouse was required by law to have an armed guard of six men flanking the front door every Sunday and Lecture Day to protect the congregation from Indian attack. It was also customary to station an armed lookout on the roof of the meetinghouse."[57] Leffingwell surely fulfilled these guard functions at times.

A town meeting was held by the citizens of Saybrook on January 4, 1648, and Thomas Leffingwell was there. By this time he was married and a landowner. This was held at the Meeting House located at what is now the corner of Church Street and Fenwick Street. On this occasion the lands beyond the immediate village of Saybrook, called "the outlands," were distributed among the people. This included an area across the Connecticut River, on the east bank, now called Lyme, and Leffingwell selected, or was given by lot, additional and larger land there.[58] Throughout his life, Leffingwell was always interested in obtaining new and more land. Over a lifetime, he owned hundreds of acres in various lots and locations.

In March of 1649/1650, the people of Saybrook had a grievance which was presented to the colonial legislature (called the "General Court"). "The petition from the Inhabitants of Saybrook," the official record stated, was "presented by Mathew Grisswold and Tho: Leppingwell." Here can be seen the use of the name "Leppingwell" instead of "Leffingwell," and perhaps reaffirming the earlier tie in his life to Michael Leppingwell back in Boston. Though they knew the context at the time, looking at the record now it is not clear just what the grievance was, except that they wanted a previous decision of the General Court to be changed. "Grisswold" and "Leppingwell" did not carry the day, however, though the Court was willing to consider it further if something new came up. "But in the meane time," the record says, the legislators "advise the petitioners to adress themselves to a ready observation of what is imposed, untill the Courte see cause to make another judgement in the case."[59] What is important here is not the issue or its result, but that young Thomas Leffingwell, only about twenty six years old, was selected as a spokesman for the townspeople. They obviously had a respect for him, and he had a manner of public presentation and speaking they thought would further their cause. In the future he would be back to the colonial legislature many times, sitting as a delegate himself.

There exists on page 25 of Saybrook Records a list of land owners in 1650. Among the names of forty people is that of Leffingwell. "The Lands of Thomas Leffingwell" included:

> 1. His house and home lot of two acres abutting north to the river and south to the marsh, and southwest to the land of Major Mason.

> 2. Fifty-five acres of upland land lying upon black hill abutting the commons.

> 3. Ten acres of marsh lying upon the eastern point lying on both sides of the creek near south cove.[60]

Coming from a background of a youth with no family, now at only twenty six years of age Thomas Leffingwell had come a long way in a short time. He was living his life day to day in Saybrook, working his lands, raising his family, and living in the world of 1600s Connecticut. On one occasion he was with three Indians when they crossed the Connecticut River together. It was a simple and ordinary thing to do, but it gives insight into the man. It demonstrates that he had an everyday familiarity with the Native Americans, and freely associated with them. The incident became memorialized for history because a Dutch merchant on a ship at Saybrook was charged with selling clothing illegally to Indians. It had nothing to do with Leffingwell, but his name was casually mentioned when the General Court considered the issue on May 15, 1651. "John Dyer testifieth in Courte, that... hee tarried there [on the river] awhile, in which time of his tarrying there came three Indians to him, and that Thomas Leppingwell was with them, which said Indians desired this deponent to sett them over in the cannoe, to Seabrooke."[61] It provides a glimpse of the past: Thomas Leffingwell, traveling with Indians.

There are other small insights of particular moments. At another Saybrook town meeting on January 7, 1655, Thomas Leffingwell is on the list of those persons in attendance.[62] A few months later, at a Court of Magistrates held on June 13, 1655, Leffingwell sued Thomas Rowell "in an Action of the Case about loss of Swyne to the Damage of 13 shillings."[63]

The Growing Leffingwell Family

Thomas Leffingwell and his wife Mary (whatever may be her true identity and origin) began their long companionship about 1647. They were probably married in the usual manner for that time and place. In the Puritan way of marrying it was encouraged that the man and woman actually be in love, and that they have an opportunity to get to know each other beforehand. There were no pre-arranged marriages. The suitor would seek the permission and approval of the prospective bride's father. The wedding was considered more of an entering into a civil contract between and a man and a woman than being a religious ceremony. The Connecticut "blue laws" at the time, which reflected the prevailing religious practice, required that "whosoever intends to joine themselves in marriage covenant shall cause theire purpose of contract to bee published in some publique place, and at some publique meeting, in the severall townes where such persons dwell, at the least, eight dayes before they enter into such contract, whereby they engage themselves each to other."[64] During the eight days of notice anyone objecting to the marriage could speak up.

After the eight days, the couple would be married in a simple civil ceremony. If Mary was the Mary White of Dorchester, Massachusetts, the wedding may have taken place there. Weddings were performed in a home. Since Thomas had no family, it probably was held in Mary's family home. Puritans made no vows and did not exchange rings. The bride and groom were simply asked whether they freely consented to the wedding. A modest celebration at the home would take place afterward.[65] The Leffingwells then made their home in Saybrook, living on the waterfront.

For people who did not have a lack of fertility, having many children was the way of life. The Leffingwells were no exception. Large families were both a blessing and a challenge. They had many children, not all of whom survived to adulthood. Children were usually christened by the pastor at the local church the Sunday following their birth, and that is probably what the Leffingwells did.

The records of Saybrook[66] have preserved the names and birth dates of the first six Leffingwell children:

1. Rachel, born 17 March 1647/1648.
2. Thomas, born 27 August 1649.
3. Jonathan, born 6 December 1650.
4. Joseph, born 24 December 1652.

5. Mary, born 10 December 1654.
6. Nathaniel, born 11 December, 1656.

There is no further record at any time concerning the boy Jonathan, so he presumably died as an infant or youth. After leaving Saybrook for Norwich, a fifth son was born:[67]

7. Samuel, born about 1662.

There was possibly another child born in Norwich, who has been left out of some accounts:

8. Deborah, born sometime between 1663 and 1674.

There is uncertainty about whether Deborah was the daughter of Thomas Leffingwell the first,[68] the subject of this book, or of his son, Thomas Leffingwell 2d. She would have been quite late to be in the family of Thomas 1st, but such things happen. On the other hand she crowds the wedding date of Thomas 2nd, whose first child was supposedly a son. This is a subject fit for its own inquiry.

The lives of the Leffingwells would have been much like that of the other people of Saybrook. They were much involved in caring for, feeding, and enjoying their growing family of young children. The social center of the community was the meeting house, which was in the Great Hall of Saybrook Fort. The people were a simple, brave, God-fearing folk, but with a very honest and cheerful determination to make the best of hard conditions.[69] Their lives centered on their families, their farms, their neighbors, and the church. Many of them had come to the New World to worship God as they saw fit and live free in a new land, and this is what they were now doing. They struggled to sustain themselves on what crops they could grow, what animals they could raise or find in the forest, and upon trade goods brought in by ship. Their beginning was doubtless impoverished but improving year by year.

By the late 1650s about half or more of the men and women in Saybrook believed they saw greener pastures and a better life on the tract of land that would become Norwich, Connecticut, about twenty-two miles to the northeast. One of the reasons for moving was the realization that a sand bar in the Connecticut River prevented deep draft ships from reaching Saybrook, limiting future trade and development. The Norwich soil was seen as more fertile for agriculture. Another reason was that cutting out new farms and homes in the wilderness was already becoming the American way of life.

By the end of 1660 the Leffingwells and the others left Saybrook behind. A decade later, Leffingwell sold his land back in the old town to his friend Matthew Griswold in a deed dated February 18, 1674.[70]

Chapter 5

Co-Founder of the Town of Norwich

In June of 1659 the sachem Uncas and his two sons, Owaneco and Attawanhood, signed a deed for nine square miles of land jointly to more than thirty proprietors, one of whom was Thomas Leffingwell. There were many notable men in this group, foremost of which were Captain John Mason and Reverend James Fitch. Leffingwell and many others were not far behind in importance. Together they formed a vital, sustainable community that became Norwich, Connecticut.

Uncas had many reasons for doing this. In part it was gratitude to Leffingwell for his rescue mission, but he was also grateful to the English in general for sustaining him and his tribe against the Narragansetts. This new settlement would put the English near the Mohegan homeland for mutual protection in case of a future war, which in fact did come. Uncas was also paid seventy pounds sterling. It must be said that this deeding of land was part of a generous - too generous - pattern of giving away Mohegan lands, something that would ultimately be to the great detriment of the tribe.

No settler fort was ever necessary to protect Norwich from hostile Indians. "The Moheagans were a great defence, and of essential service to the town for many years," wrote historian Benjamin Trumbull. "They kept out their scouts and spies, and so constantly watched their enemies, that they gave the earliest notice of their approach, and were a continual defence against them. For this purpose, in times of danger, they often moved and pitched their wigwams near the town, and were a great terror to the enemy." The place where they "pitched their wigwams" was usually on the land of Thomas Leffingwell, whose property was on the edge of town. "Once the hostile Indians came near to the town, upon the sabbath, with a design to make a descent upon it," Trumbull continued, "but, viewing it from an eminence, and seeing the Moheagan huts, they were intimidated, and went off without doing the least damage."[71]

As soon as the deed had been procured from Uncas, the lands of the new township were surveyed. Thomas Leffingwell, who had become a surveyor with a good reputation throughout the colony, would have been heavily involved in identifying and marking the town, farm, house, and street boundaries. Establishing the new town, building a new family home, laying out the new farm, and imagining their new lives, had to have been an exciting and optimistic time for Thomas and Mary Leffingwell and their young family, and all of the other Norwich settlers. Home lots were assigned later in the fall of 1659.[72] Leffingwell was in his mid-thirties, in the prime of life, with an adventurous past behind him and a great future ahead.

It took a great and cooperative effort by the Puritan community to establish itself in the new town of Norwich. Trees were cut down and the underbrush burned to make room for a town and its people. Rude initial buildings and a house of worship were erected before the arrival of the first inhabitants in the spring of 1660.

The town was laid out in a winding valley along the Yantic River, which ran generally northwest to southeast. The valley was sheltered on both sides by the sharply rising, rocky and well wooded hills. A broad street was opened through the valley, on each side of which home lots were arranged. A common town green was located at the center of town, where a church was placed at the corner.[73] The home lots were each comprised of several acres and were in general river lands, favorable for mowing, pasture and village. This was the improved soil that induced them to leave Saybrook.[74]

Leffingwell built a house on the southeast end of the town just below the summit of Sentry Hill, on what is now the southeast corner of Washington Street and Harland Road. Like most of the other houses, it was surely expanded over time from the original structure. The house lot was six acres in size, with a frontage of sixty-one rods (about a thousand feet) along the main road. There was an adjacent field of eighteen more acres for farming, but part of which was rocky.[75]

The Leffingwell land is where the Mohegans set up their wigwams near the family house. Their presence was an everyday fact of life for the family. "Sergt. Leffingwell was peculiarly the soldier and guardsman of the new town," wrote Frances Caulkins in *History of Norwich*, "and Sentry Hill was the look-out post, commanding the customary Indian route from Narragansett to Mohegan. A sentry box was built on the summit, and in times of danger and excitement, a constant watch was kept from the height. Here too, in the war with Philip, a small guard-house was built, sufficient for some ten or twelve soldiers to be housed."[76]

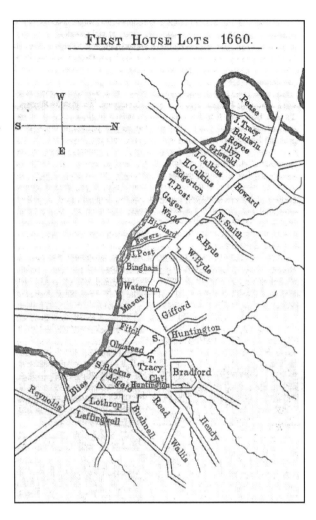

FIRST HOUSE LOTS 1660.

This map depicts the properties as owned by the original founders of Norwich. Thomas Leffingwell's land is shown at the bottom. Note that this map is turned with West being at the top, so Leffingwell was at the East end of the original town. (The map is from History of Norwich, Connecticut, by Frances Manwaring Caulkins.)

Dr. Albert Leffingwell in *The Leffingwell Record* described it this way: "This location of Mr. Leffingwell's home lot was itself significant. It fronted on an old Indian trail.... Indian wigwams were still in the occupancy of portions of the pasture lot, when he took possession. The hill to the north and east, from its earliest use became significant, bearing from several generations the name which indicated its use, 'Sentry Hill.' On this old Indian trail, grazing his cattle over this 'wigwam pasture' ground, 'Sergt. Thomas Leffingwell' begins life in his new home. The sentry station had been located, probably by his own direction, on the hill near his house."[77]

This house at the corner of Washington Street and Harland Road likely had its beginnings as the home of Thomas and Mary Leffingwell.

The Leffingwell house was probably typical of Norwich in the 1660s. "The early houses... were seldom thoroughly finished, and the upper rooms of course were cold and comfortless," Norwich historian Caulkins wrote of Leffingwell's day. The homes were unpainted, as the ubiquitous New England white paint did not come into widespread use until the 1700s. "These old houses were generally square, heavy buildings, with stone chimneys that occupied a large space in the center. The posts and rafters were of great size and solidity, and in the rooms heavy beams stood out from the ceiling overhead. The floors were made of stout plank, with a trap door leading to the cellar. A line of shelves in the kitchen... performed the office of side-table and closet.... The ceilings were low, and the fire-place, running deep into the chimney, gaped like an open cavern. But when the heaped-up logs presented a front of glowing coals and upward-rushing flame, while storms were raging without, or the heavy snow obliterated the landscape, such a fountain of warmth not only quickened the blood but cheered the heart, inspired gratitude, and promoted social festivity.... Yet these large fire-places were not without their disadvantages. They required a constant current of air from without to force the smoke up the chimney, and this kept the room cold. They were often made eight feet wide, and two or three feet deep. Wood was cut four feet in length, and the rolling in of a log... made all the timbers creak" throughout the house.[78]

Thomas Leffingwell was from the beginning of Norwich one of the most well known and liked people in town. He served in the local militia (called a "traine-band"), as a "townsman" (city councilman, in 1669, 1677, 1679, 1680, 1682, 1684 and 1686 and perhaps other years), and in the colonial legislature for many years. He made many purchases of land, and became a wealthy man for those days.[79]

Life in 1600s Connecticut

Mary Perkins, writing in Norwich in the 1890s when much of the original life in that town was still evident in the houses and streets and in the traditions of the people, brought into focus many ordinary aspects of the life that the Leffingwells would have known in the 1600s. "The home-lots of the first settlers were surrounded by high fences," she wrote, "the early law requiring that those in front should be "a five rayle or equivalent to it, and the general fence a three rayle.... These were quite necessary, on account of the free range that the cattle, sheep and swine enjoyed, the latter proving a great nuisance...."[80]

Perkins went on to describe many of the details of day to day life. Even with some unfamiliar terms to the modern reader, they present interesting images to the mind, and provide some understanding of the life of Thomas Leffingwell and his family, so are quoted at length:

> The larger houses were of two stories, generally square, with a huge central chimney, and a long roof, which, extending at the back of the house almost to the ground, formed a one story projection called the lean-to in the rear. On the first floor were generally four rooms - the "Great Room" or "Company Room," or "Keeping- Room" (as it was sometimes called), a large [bed] chamber, a kitchen, and a pantry or milk-room. On the second floor were [bed] chambers, and very often a porch chamber, which, according to the early deeds, seems to have been quite a feature of the first Norwich houses.... The doors and window shutters were fastened with huge bars of wood....

> The kitchen was the principal room, and made a cheerful gathering place for the family circle, with its rows of burnished pewter dishes on the dresser, the log seats and high settle in the chimney corner, the deep cavernous fire-place, with its imposing array of cranes, kettles, jacks, spits, pot-hooks or trammels, and the fire-dogs, on which the burning logs piled up against the huge back-log blazed far up into the chimney. Into one side of the chimney was built the oven, and over the fire-place was a high shelf, and there were recesses for books, and closets in the most

unexpected places. Hanging from the ceiling were the family stores of flitches of bacon, venison, skins of wild animals, and strings of dried apples, ears of corn and pumpkins. The floors were sanded, and... windows were of oiled paper [instead of glass].

High chests of drawers, huge carved chests, stiff old-fashioned chairs, and stools, and high-post bedsteads with hangings, formed the furniture of the other rooms. The food was plain. Samp, pounded maize, hasty puddings (or mush), succotash and yokeug, baked beans, bean-porridge and Indian pudding, were staple articles of diet. Norwich puddings were of huge size, and as famous among the local wits as New London dumplings.

The open wood-fire was for a long time the only mode of heating. There was no way of warming the churches, so that the women carried little foot stoves and the men sat with their feet incased in large leather overshoes called "boxes...."[81]

Transportation in early Connecticut, and everywhere in the colonies, was difficult, slow, and laborious. The best method of travel was by ship or canoe on the rivers or Long Island Sound, and so Saybrook and Norwich and all other early towns were built on rivers or the Atlantic Ocean. The only way of getting from place to place on land was by walking, or by horseback or horse-drawn carriage, and crude carts were used for the conveyance of goods. The early roads were rough cart-paths, or foot paths, with little attempt to keep them in order.

Mary Perkins also gives an interesting look at the clothing of the people of those days, which would have included Thomas and Mary Leffingwell and their children:

Among the early settlers, long-cloaks, hats with broad brims and steeple-crowns, and square-toed shoes with enormous buckles were worn by both sexes. The men often wore boots with short, broad tops. The doublet [a short jacket] was also used..., wearing it over a sleeved waistcoat [a vest worn over a shirt], the sleeves often slashed and embroidered. Stiffly starched ruffs, falling bands and deep linen collars, gloves with heavily embroidered and fringed gauntlets, and large breeches tied with ribbons above the knee... completed the prevailing costume for men.... Long hair...remained in fashion until superseded by the wig [in the 1700s]. Laborers wore knit caps often ornamented with a tassel, and leather clothing, though the latter was frequently worn by the better sort.[82]

It can be seen from these descriptions, and from contemporary paintings of other men, that Thomas Leffingwell likely had long hair (his own rather than a wig) with a long coat and tall hat. The Revolutionary War era image of a colonial man with a wig and a three-corner hat came later. Like everyone else, he would have spoken with the English accent he was raised with in England, probably the sound of Essex.

Class distinctions were very marked in those early days. The title of "Esq." (or "esquire") was only used by officials and persons of distinction. "Mr." was applied to clergymen, and deputies of the colonial assembly, which would have included Thomas Leffingwell starting in 1662, and those known to be of "good English descent." Only a very few men were allowed to write after their names the word "gentleman" or "gent." "Goodman" was the common term for yeomen and farmers, and "goodwife" or "goody" for their wives. The term "mistress" designated a young unmarried woman, as the title "Miss" was not used until about the mid-1700s. The office of church deacon was highly esteemed, and also the positions of captain, lieutenant, ensign, and sergeant in the local militia. Leffingwell was very often referred to in documents by his then-current rank in the militia, which we will see progressed from sergeant to ensign to lieutenant. [83]

Every town was to a large extent its own world, and had to be almost completely self-sufficient. Distance and isolation made the importation of goods difficult and expensive. Mary Perkins continued that:

> The lands must first be cleared, and the houses built. As laborers and servants were scarce, everyone must lend a hand. Each village must have its blacksmith, its cooper, weaver, shoemaker, carpenter and wheelwright, so in the new settlements the skillful mechanic always finds a warm welcome and a prosperous livelihood awaiting him. Those who have not already learned a trade, find it for their interest to do so. Young men were obliged to serve an apprenticeship, usually of seven years, ere they were considered capable of starting in business for themselves.

The early laws of Connecticut allowed "no person or householder" to "spend his time idlely or unprofittably," for the constables were instructed to "use speciall care and dilligence to take knowledge of offenders in this kind," and to bring them before the courts; so if we could have looked in upon our forefathers in the early days of Norwich, we should have found them laboring to fulfil the scriptural injunction of doing with all their might whatever their hands found to do.

Farming operations were often combined with a trade....[84]

This was true of Thomas Leffingwell. He was a farmer, but also engaged regularly in surveying, land speculation and development, being a member of the colonial legislature, and whatever else he could do to make a living.

Leffingwell's Lands: "A White Oake Markt TL"

Over the years the amount of land owned by Thomas Leffingwell became considerable in extent and diverse in nature. His holdings were listed in a book of Norwich records,[85] likely initially written in 1672 when the town authorities decided to create a registry of the lands claimed by the inhabitants.[86] These lists were later modified as ownership changes occurred. His primary properties were these:

1. "His home Lott twelve acres more or less, abuting northerly on Joseph Bushnells land seventeen rods, abuting westerly on the highway eighty six rods [about a thousand feet], abutting southeasterly on the land of Joseph Bushnell twenty rods, abutting easterly on his pasture land, being layd out November 1659."

2. "Ten acres of pasture land, abutting westerly on his home lott...."

Leffingwell obtained numerous other lots. One involved "fifty one acres of land on the east side of Quenabauge River abutting the Brooke, northeast eighty rods to a white oake markt TL...." No doubt that TL marking has long since disappeared.

Sixty three acres at Trading Cove south of town, and fifty more at the point nearby. His twenty two lands total about 640 acres, or one square mile, of Connecticut countryside. They are described in detail in Appendix B of this book. He also received another two hundred acres from Chief Uncas, and

48

had numerous other lands in Windham, Voluntown, and other locations. Thomas Leffingwell was a man of property.

The Puritan Church

Being a member of a religious community was the foremost reason most English people immigrated to Connecticut in the Great Puritan Migration. The practice was that the members of each congregation covenanted with each other to walk in "God's way." It was a community-oriented way of living, not just an individual journey. It affected every aspect of their lives.

In order to understand Thomas Leffingwell and his life, one must also have some understanding of the religion of the Puritans. It very much shaped the way he viewed the world and the way he behaved in his personal life. It is inconceivable that Thomas Leffingwell could have been such a prominent person and served in so many positions for so long without having been a church member in good standing who had a stamp of approval from the local pastor. It must be concluded that Leffingwell was in substantial agreement with prevailing Puritan attitudes and beliefs. "That he was a Christian citizen," wrote Dr. Leffingwell of his ancestor, "appears from his early connection with the church of Mr. Fitch, with whom he had come from Saybrook. He is found on the committees of the church and society, and seems to have been ready for any service to which religious duty called him."[87]

The Puritans of very early Connecticut viewed themselves as God's people, and as "a wilderness people," a phrase sometimes appearing in their legislative records. Although they came to America seeking the right to worship as they wished, there was no religious liberty except to practice their predominant brand of Puritanism. The church was supported by taxes rather than by donation of its members. Accepted protocols required the entire population to attend church services, but only a small minority earned admittance to full church membership. These church members, including Thomas Leffingwell, enjoyed considerable power and influence. They chose their own ministers and elected elders and deacons to administer the church. They voted to admit new members and to punish or dismiss those who offended against God's laws. Heretics—and that included anyone who was not a Puritan—faced fines, banishment, imprisonment, or corporal punishment.[88]

The modern Congregational Church that has descended from the Puritans has a tolerant Christian viewpoint, believing that in following Jesus Christ individuals have freedom and responsibility in matters affecting their spiritual life and experience, and that everyone has the right to exercise personal judgment in questions of belief and biblical interpretation. This was not so in the 1600s.

The Congregational Church of the Puritans was distinctly Calvinist in its beliefs. They believed in the inherent depravity of man, predestination of those chosen by God, and that God and Satan were present everywhere. They believed in following strict rules of personal behavior, including attendance at church meetings for extended sessions of preaching, instructing children in all aspects of the gospel, and keeping the Sabbath day holy. They prohibited the celebration of Christmas and Easter.

On Sundays, meetings were held both morning and afternoon with a break in between. Prayers, the singing of the Psalms and hymns, and lectures of an hour or more were part of each meeting. It was a day when everyone joined together in a common purpose. People knew each other, and about each other. There was a strong sense of community that drew in every individual.

The "Norwich Jubilee" was held in September 1859 in celebration of the two hundredth anniversary of the founding of the town. One of the speakers on that occasion, Bishop Alfred Lee of the Episcopal Church in Wilmington, Delaware, had lived in New London, Connecticut. He made some interesting observations of the religious nature of the days when Thomas Leffingwell lived and worked in Norwich:

> In its internal regulations, the newly planted town was a miniature Puritan commonwealth. The political, religious and social elements were almost blended.... The little community was very much self-governed. The observance of each precept of the decalogue [the Ten Commandments] was vindicated by the magistrate as well as enforced from the pulpit; manners as well as morals were subject to careful supervision; and some of those who... eulogize the virtues of their ancestry, might have found it quite inconvenient to have lived under their watch....

> The early planters of these New England towns were not disposed to allow liberty to degenerate into license. They came into the wilderness to frame and enjoy institutions after their own hearts. No fine theories of universal

freedom and absolute equality trammeled their legislation. They sought, indeed, an asylum for themselves in the new world, but they had no thought of opening this asylum to all comers. New citizens were not admitted without careful scrutiny, and only such additions were tolerated as would harmonize with the previous inhabitants. The settlement was a religious society as well as a body politic. It was something like a family on a large scale, bordering... on the patriarchal condition....[89]

In 1673 the tension with the Indians (other than the Mohegans) was great. A committee was appointed to oversee the building of a new meetinghouse, which consisted of Thomas Leffingwell, Thomas Tracy, and Deacon Calkins. They contracted with a man to put a new meeting house on top of the hill overlooking the green at a place now called "meeting house rocks," which has a panoramic view of the valley below. Men would take their muskets to church and a guard would stand watch.

The Still Growing Leffingwell Family

As has been seen, Thomas and Mary Leffingwell had six children in Saybrook, and they had another one or two after their arrival in Norwich. Their day to day lives were taken up with the normal activities of raising a family, doing the innumerable tasks required to successfully operate a farm and home, participating in church and in the broader community, and enjoying the company of family and friends.

When they first arrived in Norwich, their oldest child Rachel was turning fourteen years old. In the following years the first to marry was their second child, Thomas, 23, in 1672. He married Mary Bushnell, a member of the Bushnell family that had been present in Saybrook and part of the mass move to Norwich.

There would be more than forty grandchildren for Thomas and Mary Leffingwell.[90] The first was another Thomas Leffingwell, born in 1674 to Thomas 2nd and Mary Bushnell Leffingwell, and others came in 1676, 1680, 1682, 1686, 1689, 1691, 1693 and 1695. The last one, a son, died at four years of age. There is a great deal of information available on these Leffingwell descendants in *The Leffingwell Record* by Dr. Albert Leffingwell, and the reader is referred there for more details concerning the children and grandchildren.

The second daughter of Thomas Leffingwell and his wife Mary was also named Mary. Just before her 19th birthday, in November 1673, she married Joseph Bushnell. Joseph was the brother of Mary Bushnell Leffingwell, who had married Thomas 2d. In other words, two of the Leffingwell children married two of the Bushnells. Joseph and Mary Leffingwell Bushnell had eleven children, born in 1675, 1677, 1679, 1681, 1682, 1684, 1686, 1688, 1690, 1692, and 1695. It can readily be seen that once their children started marrying, Thomas and Mary Leffingwell had grandchildren added to the family at the rate of about one every year.

These marriages brought into focus the fact that there was an overabundance - perhaps one can say a veritable plethora - of family members named Thomas and Mary. The subject of this book is Thomas Leffingwell, who immigrated from England to Connecticut in the 1630s. It appears that his father was named Thomas, as were his son (1649-1723/1724), grandson (1674-1733), and great-grandson (1703-1793). The elder Thomas lived so long that for the last forty years of his life there is some confusion about which Thomas Leffingwell is being referred to in the records, father or son.

This is nothing compared to the number of Marys in the family. Thomas, the subject of this book, married a woman named Mary. If Mary Leffingwell was the Mary White of Massachusetts, the daughter of Edward and Martha White (as discussed earlier in this book) then her two brothers each married different women, both named Mary. So did Thomas Leffingwell 2d, so for forty years in Norwich there were two couples named Thomas and Mary Leffingwell. Another of the Leffingwell sons, Nathaniel, married Mary Smith. Thomas Sr. and Mary Leffingwell named one of their daughters Mary, and in 1673 she married Joseph Bushnell. Joseph and Mary Leffingwell Bushnell named their first daughter Mary. It will be no surprise that the mother of Mary Bushnell and Joseph Bushnell, a widow who had remarried, was named Mary Adgate. Thomas Leffingwell 2nd and his wife Mary named one of their daughters Mary. It would be interesting to know how, when speaking within the extended Leffingwell family, they could keep straight which Mary was being discussed.

The next to marry was the oldest Leffingwell child, Rachel, on November 24, 1681. She was then thirty-three years old, and she married Robert Parke of Stonington, Connecticut. They had ten children.

There is no record of the second Leffingwell son, Jonathan, except that he was born in Saybrook in 1650. He presumably died at a young age. Of the third son, Joseph born in 1652, the only thing known is that in 1679 he deeded some land to his brother, Thomas 2d.

The fourth son, Nathaniel, was wedded to Mary Smith on June 8, 1682. They had four children over the next ten years. Thomas Leffingwell in January of 1687 conveyed to this son "the land over the River Shawtucket at the Ferry," which is likely the land that Uncas had given as a reward for rescuing him. Nathaniel died in Norwich on September 20, 1697, leaving four young children.

The youngest son was Samuel, born just about the time of the move to Norwich. He married Hannah Dickinson on November 16, 1687. His wife died shortly after the birth of their only child in February 1690/1691, and Samuel died the following December. Their son, Samuel Leffingwell, was taken into the home of his grandparents, Thomas and Mary Leffingwell, and raised by them. Historian Mary Perkins in the 1860s wrote that the grandson Samuel was left "to the care of the grandparents, and he grew up to be the support and comfort of their old age."[91]

These deaths, though typical of large families in times of poor medical care, were surely a source of great sadness for Thomas and Mary Leffingwell. During his long life, Thomas would experience the deaths of three sons, young Jonathan in the 1650s, Samuel (and his wife Hannah) in 1691, and 40-year-old Nathaniel in 1697. Then there were the deaths of grandchildren: infant Daniel Bushnell (son of Mary) in 1681, three year old Jonathan Leffingwell (son of Nathaniel), and four year old Hezekiah Leffingwell (son of Thomas 2d), also in 1699.[92]

Thomas Leffingwell is made a Freeman

Men in the colonies at this time were generally considered "commoners," with no particular rights or vested interests in the affairs of a community. Once they had proven themselves to be men of quality and trustworthiness, they were advanced to the status of a "Freeman." It was something of considerable importance in early colonial New England. This designation was recommended by the town authorities where a man lived, but had to be approved by the legislature. It was the recognition that a man had reached full citizenship with all of its civil and political rights and responsibilities, something to be coveted and justly proud of.

The first session of the legislature under the new colonial charter in October 1662 made provision for this designation. "This Assembly doth order that for the future, such as desire to be admitted... shal present themselves with a certificate under the hands of the major part of the Townesmen where they live, [stating] that they are persons of civill, peaceable and honest conversation, and that they attained the age of twenty one yeares and have 20 pounds estate." Just in case this designation of status was not afterward honored by the person receiving it, it could be revoked. "And in case any freeman shal walke scandalously or commit any scandalous offence, and be legally convicted thereof, he shal be disfranchized by any of the civill Courts."[93]

In May of 1671 the legislature considered eight men from the town of Norwich to be made Freemen. One of them was Thomas Leffingwell. "This Court accepts those propownded for freemen... and they are to be sworne by the respective... Commissioners in the towne where they dwell."[94] There is no doubt that this was a momentous occasion for these men and for their families.

The General Court had mandated that the Oath of a Freeman be taken by each person,[95] so each one of the Norwich men would have done so. Because no originals or copies have survived to the present day, the exact content of the specific oath in Connecticut is not known. However, it would have been substantially similar to the oath prescribed in Massachusetts in 1634, the wording of which was as follows, modified to insert the name of Thomas Leffingwell:

The Oath of a Freeman

I, Thomas Leffingwell, being, by Gods providence, an inhabitant & ffreeman within the jurisdiction of this comonweale, doe freely acknowledge my selfe to be subject to the goverment thereof, & therefore doe heere sweare, by the greate & dreadfull name of the everlyving God, that I wil be true & faithfull to the same, & will accordingly yeilde assistance & support thereunto, with my person & estate, as in equity I am bound, & will also truely indeavr to mainetaine & preserve all the libertyes & previlidges thereof, submitting my selfe to the wholesome lawes & orders made & established by the same; and furthr, that I will not plott nor practise any evill aginst it, nor consent to any that shall soe doe, but will timely discovery & reveale the same lawfull authority nowe here established, for the speedy preventing thereof.

> Moreover, I doe solemnly binde myselfe in the sight
> of God, that when I shalbe called to give my voice touching
> any such matter of this state, wherein ffreemen are to deale
> I will give my vote & suffrage, as I shall judge in myne owne
> conscience may best conduce & tend to the publique weale
> of the body, without respect of persons, or favr of any man.
> Soe helpe mee God in the Lord Jesus Christ.[96]

Thomas Leffingwell had come a long way. From having possibly been an orphan in England and a youth without family or fortune among the Indians and soldiers in frontier Connecticut, to now being a Freeman of Norwich, was a major accomplishment.

It appears that even before this action, Leffingwell was already considered to be a Freeman. A survey of all the freemen in all the towns in the colony was conducted, including a list of the freemen in Norwich on October 9, 1669. The names of the principal men of the town were stated, including "Thomas Leffingwell."[97] This suggests that the submission of his name for approval in 1671 was a ratification of a previous action that had been taken at the local level.

Indian Language Interpreter

On May 15, 1685, Leffingwell attended a court in Hartford which considered whether a Native American called Black James had in earlier years conveyed land to the Massachusetts Bay Company. The record of that case is important because it contains these words: "Capt. Samuel Mason, Lnt. Thomas Leffingwell & John Morgan *being interpreters*, there being Capt. Cassacinimon [the Pequot chief], Owaneco [the Mohegan chief] & John the Indian preacher & many other principall Indians of note present."[98] This trial definitely establishes that Leffingwell was fluent in the Indian language.

Chapter 6

A Witch Trial and a Hanging for Incest

There were two events in the 1660s and 1670s, one involving witchcraft in Saybrook and the other incest in Norwich, which reflected some of the darker sides of Puritanism and formed part of the life experience of Thomas Leffingwell. He knew the people involved, and surely followed these developments with the greatest interest. In the end, both stories had personal consequences to him and his family.

Witches in Saybrook

It is well known in history that in the 1690s in Salem, Massachusetts, unfortunate people, primarily women, were caught up in accusations of practicing witchcraft, and executed by stern Puritan courts. What is less remembered is that more than thirty years earlier witch hysteria swept through colonial Connecticut, which also resulted in accusations and executions.

Given the wrong combination of attitudes and events, every age and society is subject to spinning out of control. This is as true of modern society (such as with the Holocaust) as it is of ancient. It can happen anywhere that the mix of toxic elements reaches a critical mass. So it was in Connecticut about 1660.

Hysteria about witchcraft did not start in Connecticut, but came from England and continental Europe. It was part of the age. From the 1400s through 1650, thousands of people were put to death as witches. Over a fifty year period the province of Alsace, France, alone had close to five thousand executions.[99] The phenomenon wasn't just confined to the Puritans.

In New England in the 1600s there existed a pervasive religiosity with a strong belief in society that God, angels, and evil spirits were everywhere, and were to be found in the churches, in the homes, and in the farms and forests. They actively enticed people to do good or evil. There prevailed a belief that witches existed, that specific people were witches, and that they should be killed for it. Puritan leadership believed that this was supported in the Old Testament of the Bible in Exodus 22:18 ("Thou shalt not suffer a witch to live."), in Leviticus 20:27 ("A man also or woman that hath a familiar spirit, or that is a wizard, shall surely be put to death."), and in Deuteronomy 18:10 ("There shall not be found among you any one that... useth divination, or an observer of times, or an enchanter, or a witch.").

There being no separation of church and state in those days, these scriptures formed the basis of a Connecticut law requiring that if "any man or women bee a witch, that is, hath or consulteth with a familiar spirritt, they shall bee put to death."[100] This was no joking matter. Just fifty miles away from Saybrook, in the town of Windsor, Alse (Alice) Young was hanged[b] for being a witch in 1647, followed by Lydia Gilbert in 1654. In Wethersfield, Mary Johnson was executed a year later, and John and Joan Carrington four years later. In Fairfield, Goodwife Bassett ("goodwife" being the title for married women before use of the term "Mrs.") was hanged in 1651, and Goodwife Knapp in 1653. Nicholas Bailey and his wife in New Haven were acquitted of witchcraft but still banished from the town.[101]

It is worthwhile to seek to understand how such things could happen in the world of Thomas Leffingwell. The common elements causing witch hysteria were community and economic stress in a pervasively religious local area, with an accusing finger pointed at a socially marginal middle-aged woman (and sometimes a man as well), who had troubled relations with neighbors in which threats were made.[102] Personal eccentricities boosted suspicions and distrust.

The situation in Saybrook was ripe for group hysteria and the accusation that certain people were practicing witchcraft. Puritanism and belief in evil spirits were well established. The coming abandonment of Saybrook by so many people moving to Norwich, which was something of a social collapse, was one of the ingredients that went into the cauldron that soon came to a boil. The stress in 1659 was severe. Half of the people in town, including Thomas Leffingwell and his family, were leaving as soon as they could the following year. Those that remained were either uninvited to the new town of Norwich, or did not want to go. The impact of that departure, both as the move was planned and then as it was carried out, was negative for the people who remained. They were losing their friends, neighbors, population, land value, and their only pastor. "To the Puritan mind the devil

---

[b]The proper English grammar is that pictures are hung but people are hanged.

was amongst them at all times, looking for opportunity," one historian has written, and some believed that Satan was "working hard to destroy their fledgling community by enticing its settlers to move away."[103]

Nicholas and Margaret Jennings were the Saybrook residents who fell victim to the colonywide witch mania. In that very small town Thomas Leffingwell would have known them and about them, and also would have known their accusers.[c]

The Jennings couple had a disfavored history. Nicholas was the son of a lower class chimney sweep in Hartford, and as an adult moved to New Haven where he met Margaret Bedford. She was an indentured servant, and the two ran away together in 1642. They were caught and brought back, and she may have been pregnant. He was convicted of fornication and whipped. She was convicted of fornication and of stealing household goods from Captain Nathaniel Turner, the man to whom she had been indentured. She was ordered to be whipped and to marry Jennings. Nicholas had to serve out Margaret's term of indenture to Turner, and to pay double the value of the things she took. A sign of possible witch power occurred three years later when Turner was mysteriously lost at sea when his ship sank on a voyage to England.

The couple moved to Hartford, where in 1647 Nicholas Jennings was convicted of beating another man's cow. Then they moved to Saybrook, where Jennings bought land next to Captain John Mason. Jennings had fought in the Pequot War under Mason, just as Leffingwell had, and the two had very likely known each other during the war. Now Jennings acquired land adjacent to Mason, just as Leffingwell had, making the three families neighbors.

After the passage of twelve years things were going badly again for the Jennings family. Margaret and Nicholas were accused of using witchery that caused the death of Marie Marvin, the wife of Reinold Marvin. She supposedly died from a spell or other adverse effect of witchcraft. The Marvins were the aunt and uncle of Mary Marvin Bushnell Adgate, a well known woman in town and the wife of Thomas Adgate.

---

[c]There is an informative discussion of the Jennings couple and the witchcraft situation in the pamphlet *Saybrook's Witchcraft Trial of 1661* by Donald Perreault.

The public records show that suspicions of witchcraft in Saybrook were swirling. "Mr. Willis [of the colonial government] is requested to goe downe to Sea Brook, to assist the Major [Mason] in examininge the suspitions about witchery," the public records stated on June 15, 1659, "and to act therein as may be requisite."[104] That colonial officials would participate in a witch inquiry speaks volumes about their mindset and the nature of the times. One can only imagine the discussions that went on in this investigation, the allegations of witchcraft, the evidence to support it, and the beliefs that the people had on this subject.

The investigation did ultimately result in court proceedings. The underlying factual details of the charges and the proceedings of the trial have been lost, but the indictment of Nicholas has been preserved:

> Nicholas Jennings thou art here indicted... for not having the fear of God before thine eyes, thou has entertained familiarity with Satan the great Enemy of God and mankind, and by his help hast done works above the course of nature, to the loss of the lives of several persons and in particular the wife of Reinold Marvin and the child of Balthazar de Wolfe, with other sorceries, for which, according to the law of God and the established laws of this common wealth, thou deservest to die.[105]

Margaret Jennings was similarly charged in the same sort of language. On September 5, 1661, they entered pleas of not guilty. A jury trial was held in Hartford on October 9th, with three judges and ten jurors. After hearing the evidence and deliberating for a time, the verdicts of a divided jury were returned as follows:

> Respecting Nicholas Jennings, the jury return that the major part find him guilty of the indictment, the rest strongly suspect it that he is guilty.

> Respecting Margaret Jennings, the jury return that some of them find her guilty, the rest strongly suspect her to be guilty of the indictment.

In this manner they were found not guilty of the charges, but neither were they found innocent. The death penalty could not be imposed, yet they were harshly dealt with nonetheless. Their two sons, John and Joseph, were taken from them and apprenticed out, one to an innkeeper and the other to a magistrate. "Thus, in the end the Saybrook Witchcraft Trial of 1661 is more than the story of Nicholas and Margaret Jennings," summarized historian Donald Perreault. "It is the story of a community's fear for its future. Nicholas and Margaret Jennings were merely the scapegoats of a panicked community that had reached a breaking point."[106]

Thomas Leffingwell, like all the residents of that small town, personally knew the people involved in the case. It would be interesting to know what he thought of it. It was a sad affair. By the time the trial was actually held Leffingwell and many other Saybrook residents had moved on to Norwich, but he and they knew the people involved back in the old home town, and were surely most interested in what was happening there.

Eleven years later in 1672, Thomas Leffingwell 2d married Mary Bushnell, the daughter of Mary Adgate and her first husband. This brought the initial victim in the case (Mary Bushnell Leffingwell's great-aunt, Marie Marvin) within the family. Then Thomas Leffingwell's daughter, Mary, married Mary Adgate's son, Joseph Bushnell. Stated another way, one person supposedly murdered by the witches was the great-aunt of two of his future children-in-law.

The Saybrook witch trial was followed a decade later by the trial of Thomas Rood for incest, something even more tragic and which involved the Leffingwell family far more deeply.

The Trial of Thomas Rood for Incest

Like many of the early Norwich settlers, Thomas Rood (sometimes spelled Rhood or Roode) and his wife Sarah had first been in Saybrook. They had a large family of eleven children, and were involved in the community as full fledged members of society. No doubt Thomas and Mary Leffingwell were saddened, along with the rest of the community, when Sarah Rood died in March 1668 at about 39 years of age.[107] Perhaps having so many children had taken its toll, or she may have fallen victim to a frontier disease for which there was insufficient help at that time.

Thomas Rood remained single in the following years, raising the family without a wife. His oldest daughter, an unmarried young woman also named Sarah, helped out with the children. This was where things went awry. In early 1672, 23-year-old Sarah could no longer hide that she was single and pregnant. When authorities questioned her about the identity of the baby's father, she said that it was her own father, Thomas Rood.

This caused a sensation in Puritan Norwich and in Connecticut. Father and daughter were both arrested on charges of incest. "Thomas Rhood," said the indictment, "thou art indicted... for not haveing the feare of God before thine eyes, thou hast committed that abominable sin of incest haveing carnall copulation with Sarah Rhood, thy reputed daughter, for which according to the law of God & the law of this colony thou deservest to dye."[108]

It was the same for young Sarah. "Sarah Rood," the document stated, "thou are Indicted... for not having the Fear of God before thine eyes, thou hast commited that abominable sin of Incest haveing carnall copulation with Thomas Rhood, thy reputed father, for which according to the law of God & the law of this colony thou deservest to dye."

A problem for the court was that incest wasn't prohibited by any particular law of the colony. The offense had been inadvertently left out of the code. There was no separation of church and state, and the catch-all statute was that if an act that should be illegal was not covered by the written laws of the colony then "we should have recourse to the word of God for our lawe." The local court therefore asked for guidance from Puritan ministers about what kind of sentence they should impose. The four ministers to whom inquiry was made answered that the penalty for incest was death, to be imposed upon both father and daughter.[109] This answer was not a surprise as adultery was already a capital offense, and incest was so much the worse.

Yet the trial court judges were still not so sure about the recommended penalty. This was a very grim business and the judges were uneasy. They also asked the legislature for its advice. It answered that "seeing the word of God doth anex death to be the penalty of Incest," then they, "haveing considered the case declared their judgments to be that such persons as are proved to be guilty of Incest, they ought by the lawe of God and our lawes as now they stand to be put to death."[110] What they saw as the law of God and the penalty of God, was therefore made the law and penalty of Connecticut. Thomas Leffingwell was in attendance as a delegate to the legislature when that issue came before the General Court. Dissenting votes were not generally noted in the official records, and none were recorded here. Presumably, "haveing considered the case," he voted for the response with the other legislators, in favor of death.

Thomas Rood and his daughter Sarah were tried at the "Court of Assistants" in Hartford on October 8, 1672. The defendants both simply told the truth, admitted that the charge was true, and plead guilty. There was nothing else the "Jury of Life & Death" could do but find them guilty on these pleas. The Court judges then sentenced Thomas Rood, ordering that "thou art to goe from here to the place from whence thou camest [Norwich] & and in due time to be carryed from thence to the place of execution, & there to be hanged by the neck till thou art dead, & then taken down & buried."

The date for death was set to be in just ten days, on October 18th. On the appointed day in the town of Norwich, in the view of any of his neighbors who attended the sight, 46-year-old Rood was hanged until he was dead. With his status as a public official in Norwich, it seems likely that Thomas Leffingwell was present. Thomas Rood was the first, last, and only man in colonial and American history to ever be executed for incest.

But what was to be done with the daughter, Sarah? She was pregnant with child. Ought she also to be executed? The damning fact for her was that she was 23 years old and not a mere youth. The three court judges were in turmoil. Some of them were "not fully sattisfyed... so as to concur in the passing of [a] sentence of death upon her." She was ordered to be kept in custody while her sentence was being considered.

Sometime late in 1672 Sarah Rood gave birth to the child. It was a boy, and she named him George Rood. On May 19, 1673, the court met again to deal with the punishment of the daughter. The judges decided to extend mercy. "This court considering of [the] Sarah Rood case," it ruled, "doe take notice of a great appearance of force layd up upon her spirit by her father overawing & Tirancial abuse of his parentall authority, besides his bodily striveings, which not only at first brought her into the same but allso in after yielding to his Temptation and consealment of the fact." The court found that Sarah was "so ignorant & weake in minde" and that these facts "doe render her not equally Guilty." The concluded that "the father's fault was much aggravated so the child's is exceedingly mittigated."

The sentence of the judges, then, spared her from hanging, but ordered that "shee shall be severly whipt on the naked body, once at Hartford & once at Norwich." The reason, they explained, was *"so that others may heare & fear & do no more such abominable wickednesse."*[111] [Emphasis added.] So once again the people of Norwich were subjected to another display of public punishment, this time to witness the severe whipping of a young mother. Again, because he was one of the leaders of the community, it seems likely that Thomas Leffingwell was present when the punishment was applied.

Thomas and Sarah Rood, husband and wife, were both now deceased, so their numerous orphaned children became a public concern. New London County ordered the town of Norwich to have the children "placed out into sum orderly families where they may bee well Educated." Under the order they were to be raised in proper homes, and in fact they were taken in by different local families and cared for until adulthood. Besides Sarah the younger, the Roods had ten children that needed placement and supervision. This was a big order for a small town, but the people of Norwich rose to the occasion. Thomas Leffingwell and Thomas Adgate were appointed to deal with the lands and property of the deceased father to make sure that it was used to support the children, and to be available for them when they attained adulthood. The Rood children eventually received the lands their father had owned, and some of them stayed in Norwich as adults.

The younger Sarah continued on for a time as the single mother of her son, George, in New London. Evidently things did not go well. Just before his third birthday in 1675 a new order was made. "Upon the motion of Thomas Leffingwell," the court recorded, "the Court orders that Lefft. Leffingwell shall keepe the child of Sarah Rood till he hath attained the age of 21 years, or have liberty to put the child to some other person as the mother of the child & he shall agree."[112]

This was a momentous order. At Thomas Leffingwell's own request, he and his wife took the three year old boy, George Rood, into their home. They raised him in their family for many years to come, until he legally became a man. Thomas and Mary, then, bore the ultimate impact of incest, which was the burden of supporting and raising this boy in their own home.

Why was this order made? Why was Thomas Leffingwell the one to take in the child? It has been said- rumored - that the Leffingwells and the Roods were related. There seems to be only one basis for this statement, and that is a casual remark by Frances Caulkins in her extensive book *History of Norwich.* In that work she never mentioned this infamous incest case of Thomas Rood, perhaps because it was too improper of a subject to be dealt with in 1866. (Nor was it mentioned in the 1790s by Jonathan Trumbull, or in the 1890s by either Mary Perkins or Dr. Albert Leffingwell.) Caulkins does, however, mention some of the children of the Rood marriage, and in doing so dropped a comment that pertains directly to the issue of a family tie. "John, son of Thomas and Sarah Rood of Norwich, had a home-lot granted him in 1679," she said, "on the other side of Showtucket river, near to his *uncle Leffingwell's.*"[113] [Emphasis added.]

The statement has nothing to do with George Rood, but if Leffingwell was an uncle to John Rood he would also have been the uncle to John's half-brother George. This comment seems to be the only place in history where Leffingwell was said to be the Rood children's uncle, at least before the internet enabled unsubstantiated claims to be instantly spread across cyberspace. No contemporary document supports the proposition that Thomas Leffingwell was the uncle of the Rood children. The order giving him custody of the child said nothing about any family relationship.

"Uncle" is a word that may be applied in a strict blood relation sense, or in a loose sense of familiarity and endearment. It is an imprecise word. Caulkins, however, two hundred years after the event, made an offhanded reference to his being an uncle, but without citation to the source of the information. It is very possible, maybe even likely, that Caulkins was simply stating her own conclusion as though it were a fact.

It is untenable to say that Thomas Leffingwell *must* have been an uncle of George Rood because he requested the custody order that was given. The other Rood children were parceled out under an earlier order to different families which took them in, not because they were relatives but because they were trying to do a Christian act of charity and help the community with young people in great need. It wasn't until the final child that Leffingwell acted. If he was the uncle of all of them, it seems he would have been the first to act, not the last. This is not said to diminish the value of what he did, but to analyze the claim that he was an uncle.

There are unsupported claims made on online family history sites that since Thomas Leffingwell was the uncle of George Rood, then the mother Sarah Rood must have been his sister. They give her the name Sarah Leffingwell Rood. No such person, or relationship to Thomas, can be shown to have ever existed. Another direction of speculation is that Thomas Leffingwell's wife, Mary, and Sarah Rood were sisters. This has no historical basis. Even further afield from evidence is the apparent fantasy that Mary and Sarah were the daughters of Uncas.

Sometimes historical evidence is much less interesting than historical rumors. A more likely explanation is that Thomas Leffingwell was simply a good man and that Mary was a good woman, and they acted not because they were relatives, but because they were big hearted and willing to welcome into their home a hapless and innocent three year old boy. Sixteen years later, they would also take into their family their newly orphaned two-year-old grandson, Samuel Leffingwell 2d.

The Rood tragedy did not end here. Living in the home of the Leffingwells was the bright time in the life of George Rood, but he ran into more severe troubles years later. In July 1702 he married 20-year-old Hannah Bush. It turned out that she was already pregnant, but not with the child of George. The father of her child was her step-father, Thomas Hall, who had repeatedly raped her.

Magistrate Richard Bushnell (the brother of two of Thomas Leffingwell's children-in-law) had Hall arrested, along with Hannah's mother, Susannah, who was considered complicit with Hall in the wrongdoing. In fact, the mother confessed that she had forced the daughter to have sex with the step-father. Hall denied it. Then Susannah changed her story and said that when she confessed she "was bewiched for I felt my strength and senses faild me," and now said that Hall was actually innocent.

Thomas Hall and his wife Susannah were charged with incest and accessory to incest. After the shock of the execution of Thomas Rood thirty years earlier, the laws had been changed to remove the death penalty from sex crimes. The Halls were found guilty and sentenced to stand at the gallows with a rope around their necks for one hour, receive a whipping not to exceed forty lashes, and wear a capital letter "I" two inches tall and in contrasting color, for the rest of their lives.

For her part, the young and pregnant Hannah was found guilty of concealing the crime. She was publicly whipped in Norwich. George Rood found himself battered by incest at his birth and again at his marriage. We can only try to imagine the feelings of his adoptive parents, Thomas and Mary Leffingwell, now approaching eighty years old, as they saw George's wife, Hannah, whipped before their neighbors.[114]

Amazingly, the young couple seem to have survived this initial disaster to their marriage and went on to success. They stayed together, lived and worked in Norwich, and raised eight children of their own. Thomas Leffingwell gave them land to start off their married lives together. In those days many girls were named with hoped-for personal virtues, such as Faith, Patience, Prosper, Temperance, Prudence, and Obedience. Interestingly, one of the daughters of George and Hannah was named Experience Rood, and another Thankful Rood.

These stories of witches and incest illustrate a part of the world in which Thomas Leffingwell lived, and touched his life personally.

Chapter 7

Delegate to the Connecticut Colonial Legislature

The colonial legislature of Connecticut was called the "General Court and Assembly," and in the 1600s was usually called the "General Court." It met twice a year in May and October, plus in occasional special sessions, to deal with issues of colony-wide importance. It was in some ways much like a modern state legislature, but was simpler due to the small population and the limited government of the day. Unlike today, it also dealt with the supervision of military defense, relations with Native Americans, and the supervision of churches.

A royal charter for Connecticut was granted by King Charles II in 1662, formalizing the legality of the colony and granting extensive rights of self-government. A colonial government had existed in Connecticut prior to this time, but it did not have the sanction or security of official approval as was now provided. When the General Court met in Hartford on October 9, 1662, it established a permanent government by accepting the new charter and passing a broad range of laws. It was a new legal start in Connecticut, and Thomas Leffingwell was present as a delegate from Norwich. Leffingwell had been there in the 1630s when the initial Connecticut settlers arrived, and now he was again present at the creation of the new colonial government twenty five years later. Individual delegate votes were not recorded, but his presence at the legislative session establishes that he was involved in the discussions and voting that occurred.[115]

Each town elected two delegates for the spring session and again for the fall session of the General Court, potentially four different people each year. These men received only a small per diem that covered their expenses but were not paid enough to make money an inducement to serve. The reward for being in the legislature was in the satisfaction of doing public service, the excitement of being in the middle of current events, and the prestige of the position.[116]

Thomas Leffingwell's involvement in the General Court for Norwich became a regular part of early Connecticut government over the next forty years. There were three components in his participation. He wanted to serve, he was able to serve, and the people wanted him to serve. It speaks of the esteem in which he was held by his neighbors to see that they elected him for most of the years from 1662 to 1701, where he attended fifty three regular and special sessions of the legislature. In this position he was involved in the colony-wide events during those years, the most important of which was the attempt of King James II to end the Connecticut government and replace it with a Dominion of New England dictatorship under Governor Edmund Andros.

Thomas Leffingwell served in these Fifty-Three Legislative Sessions of the Connecticut General Court

1662	Oct 09			
1662/63	Mar 10	Oct 8		
1663/64	Mar 10			
1665	Oct 12			
1668	Oct 8			
1669	Oct 14			
1670	May 12	Oct 13		
1671	May 11	Oct 12		
1672	May 9	June 26	Oct 10	
1673	May 8			
1674	May 14	Oct 8		
1676	May 11	Oct 12		
1677	May 10			
1679	May 8			
1681	Oct 13			
1682	May 11	Oct 12		
1683	May 10	Oct 11	Nov 14	
1684	Oct 9			
1685	May 14	Oct 8		
1686	May 13	July 6	July 28	Oct 14
1687	May 12	June 15	Oct 13	Oct 31
1689	May 9	Jun 13	Sep 3	
1690	May 8	Oct 9		
1691	May 14	July 9	Oct 8	
1693	May 11	Sep 1	Oct 12	
1695	Oct 10			
1696	May 14			

Miscellaneous Legislative Issues

After the initial meeting of the General Court in October 1662, Norwich sent other delegates to sessions in May of 1663, but Leffingwell was back in his legislative seat on October 9th of that year. He was listed in the record that session as "Thomas Leppingwell."[117]

Over the years Thomas Leffingwell was involved with a great many routine legislative actions across the broad spectrum of colonial life. Many items were repetitive and routine, but at times more unusual or interesting items came up, some of which will be considered here because they help the understanding of the world in 1600s Connecticut in which Thomas Leffingwell lived on a day to day basis. The items mentioned here all occurred at legislative sessions when he was in attendance.

In the October 1663 session the General Court was feeling good about life in Connecticut, and thankful for the blessings the people had received. "This Court orders," it proclaimed, "that the last Wednesday of this Instant October be set apart throughout this Collony for a solemn day of Thanksgiving for the mercyes God hath extended to us the year past" including "the plentifull harvest, the seasonable abatement of the waters, and continuance of peace and health amongst us."[118] Thanksgiving was a regular fall occurrence, starting in the very early days of Puritan history.

The plight of two women who had been deserted or widowed came before the General Court at different times. On October 14, 1669, it heard the case of Hannah Huitt of Stonington, whose husband had disappeared eight years before and had never afterward been heard from. Thomas Leffingwell and the other delegates voted that she "is at liberty to marry if shee see cause."[119]

Five years later, in October 1674, another woman was in a similar plight. "Mary Dowe, of Hartford, informeing this Court that her husband being gon to sea and not being heard of for near two yeares, and leaving her destitute of supplyes necessary for the mayntenance of herselfe and children, she is fallen into debt and knowes not how to pay the same without it be by the sale of her house and lott, and therefore desired this Court to impower her so to doe," the records state. The delegates were symphathetic, and found "good reason to grant her desire, and doe accordingly give her full power to grant, bargain and sell the sayd house and lott, and her deed therein shall be esteemed good and valid in the law."[120]

Unusual for the time, the legislature granted a divorce to Elizabeth Rogers in October 1676. "This Court haveing considered the petition of Elizabeth Rogers, the wife of John Rogers, for a release from her conjugall bond to her husband, with all the allegations and proofes presented to clear the righteousness of her desires, doe find just cause to grant her desire, and doe free her from her conjugall bond to the sayd John Rogers."[121]

In the wilderness frontier of the 1600s, such simple items as establishing the actual weight that is attributed to one ounce or one pound, and the measure of what is an actual inch, foot or yard, were not easily determined with accuracy. At the October 1670 legislative session it was noted that since "Mr. Richards hath procured waightes and measures for the use of the Colony, from England," these official standards were ordered to be implemented throughout Connecticut.

Another item of action that session involved the ordering of men in Connecticut to perform a day of work. "For the incouragement of rayseing sheep," it was voted by the delegates, "this Court orders that every male person... from fowerteen yeares old and upwards (that is not a publique officer...) shall worke one day in the year, some time in June yearly, in cutting down and clearing the underwood, that so there may be pasture; and the townesmen in the respective townes are to appoynt the dayes for this worke...." Failure to do the work would result in a fine.[122]

At a later legislative session in May 1673 the issue of sheep came up again. Maintaining the purity and vitality of the sheep was very much in the public interest. "Whereas... experience doth shew that the breed of sheep is much decayed by reason of a neglect of breeding suitable ramms and not seasonably separating them from the flocks," the legislature found, "it is ordered by this Court that two or three meete persons in each plantation shall be appoynted to take care that a suitable number of such ramms be kept in each towne, and that none be suffered to runn upon the [town] comons with the ewes, from the first of August untill the last of October...."[123]

Keeping good relations with the Indians was an important goal of the legislature. English and Native American lands were intermixed and cultural differences provided many opportunities for negative contacts between the peoples. Leffingwell was not a delegate in October 1679 when an issue came up, but his good standing with Uncas and the Mohegans caused the General Court to appoint him to be part of the solution.

The problem was that "there is complaint that the Indians receive much damage by the English cattell, which is sayd by the English to be by the badness of their fence." Native American property, crops and personal belongings were being spoiled and disrupted by the English cattle roaming onto their lands. The Indians blamed the English for letting their cattle run loose, and the English blamed the Indians for having bad fences. The legislature took action, having the fences inspected for adequacy and authorizing that errant cattle be impounded. It "ordered that there be fence veiwers and appraisers appoynted in each towne... to apprize what damages shal be done in the Indians' corne by any English cattell, swine or horses... and the Indians are allowed to make pownds within their own feilds to secure and imprison such horses, cattell, swine, as they find trespassing; and they are to give speedy notice to the townesmen... of what horses, cattell or swine are impownded by them.... Lnt [Lieutenant] Tho: Leffingwell and John Allyn are appoynted to be fence veiwers for the Mohegen feilds...."[124] In fulfilment of this assignment, Leffingwell would have gone out and inspected the Mohegan fences, walking them with John Allyn and probably Uncas or perhaps some other Native American, checking them for sufficiency to keep out cattle.

On occasion Leffingwell was appointed to perform administrative functions for the legislature. He was more than once designated as part of a committee to audit the Treasurer's accounts,[125] and the record shows that "Lnt. Leffingwell is appoynted and impowered to administer the oath of a Commissioner" to an individual.[126]

One of the things that is evident when reading the minutes of the General Court in the 1600s is that the legislature approved a great many land grants. These varied in size from a few acres or hundreds to even more than a thousand acres. There is no evident consciousness among the delegates that Connecticut was a small colony, or that land was a limited resource for a growing population, or that one day every acre would be of great use and value. It appears that they viewed the land as having an unlimited supply.

Surveying for the Legislature

In the records of Connecticut there are a great many deeds that bear witness that Thomas Leffingwell lived. He bought and sold his own lands, and prepared legal descriptions for others. Surveying was a significant activity in his life. It is not known how he acquired the skill, but it was a most useful one in the unchartered wilderness of 1600s Connecticut. He was doing original work where no surveyor had ever set foot before, marking off wilderness for the first time. As more and more people came into the colony, and land was divided and then re-divided, it was essential to establish reliable property boundaries. It was a helpful occupation to Leffingwell and his family, providing extra cash or goods as compensation for his services. He taught his sons how to survey, and he and they would make much use of the skill.

The legislature frequently appointed surveyors to lay out the boundaries of land it had granted, or approved for transfer, or in order to settle a dispute between landowners. It used different men for each area of the colony, and Leffingwell was a frequent appointee for eastern Connecticut. The General Court would designate two men to do a survey, and afterward pay them for their work. It is recorded that at the General Court session on March 10, 1663/1664, another surveyor should be paid "what is his due, at 3 shillings a day, himself & horse."[127] Presumably, this is what Thomas Leffingwell was paid, though we do not know how much that value is in modern money. It was enough to induce the surveyors to take the time to do the work.

An example of these appointments occurred at the General Court session held in Hartford on October 8, 1668. The Court that session appointed him, along with his old Saybrook friend Matthew Griswold, to survey a two hundred acre grant of land for James Rogers near New London.[128] This became a very common occurrence over the next thirty five years, with the General Court appointing Thomas Leffingwell and a second person, often Thomas Tracy, to work as a team to survey a line or property description.

Accurate surveying, then and now, prevents social chaos by establishing proper and accurate boundaries. Ambiguous borders with disputed ownership creates trouble, but when people know exactly where their property line is they can be good neighbors. The problem, of course, is in being accurate.

Thomas Leffingwell lived before all modern surveying systems had been invented, and before the Public Land Survey System of township, range, and section had been devised. He used a method of description that could be called a true "metes and bounds" system. A typical survey would include references to a nearby creek, the nearby farmer's property, a particularly large tree, the adjoining road, a large boulder, or other distinguishing natural feature.

The method of describing the boundaries of land used by Thomas Leffingwell and the other surveyors reflected the standards of the time. He and Thomas Tracy reported the following description back to the legislature in 1676:

> "Wee whose names are underwritten being appoynted by the Generall Court in October, '76, to measure the bounds of Hermon Garrad's land lyeing on the east of Stoneington bounds, first, we begun to run the line at the west side of Wequatucksett brooke, a little eastward from the old forte, and so ran east northeast one mile to a pond called Pahcupog, and from thence one mile and a halfe north to a hill called Masshattaneeseck, and from thence two miles and a halfe north northeast to Shannuck River, the place called Paychaiossuck where we marked a tree with five notches on the sowth of the river, and there was yet one mile more to measure, but the River being full that we could not pass over and forced to leave the worke. November, '76. Thomas Tracey, Thomas Leffingwell.[129]

This description gives a vision of Leffingwell and Tracy slogging through rivers, creeks, swamps, thickets, bushes and trees, setting a straight line along each distance, riding horses where they could, and walking or wading where they must. On this occasion, the river was more than they could deal with.

Almost twenty years later Leffingwell was assigned to identify a boundary line between the two towns of Preston and Stonington. It is fortunate that the colonial records preserved the very interesting report submitted by Leffingwell and John Post in October 1695:

> "We whose names are underwritten being appoynted and ordered by the Generall Court to finish the runing of the north line of Stoneington and the south of Preston from station to station, we, begining at the norwest corner of Stonington bownds runing neer est and east sowth east lyne untill we came up to the top of a mountain wher the line run throug a queach [a dense thicket] of young stadles [an early word for saplings or young trees], from thence runing untill the lyne crost a cart path which is caled the cedar swamp path, and there we marked two trees with the markes facing one against the other, the one a black oake

73

and the other a white oake: thence runing to Preston five mile corner tree which is a black oake marked on two sides standing between two rocks, and from thence runing that poynt to a chestnut tree which stands by the side of a cedar swamp being neer the corner. Thomas Leffingwell, John Post."[130]

Again we see the method of description sufficient for that day. Of course, no one can use these descriptions today to identify exactly where that tree with the five notches on the south side of the river is located, or where that line is on the ground. New surveys would have to be re-done in the future as the need arose and science progressed, and later advancements in surveying have made descriptions much more reliable and identifiable.

Thomas Leffingwell was appointed by the colonial legislature to do surveys on numerous occasions. A list of them from 1669 to 1695 is set forth in Appendix C of this book. Sometimes he surveyed the boundaries between individual people, other times between one town and another, and on occasion between Indian lands and English communities. From these assignments can be seen the fact that Thomas Leffingwell was a well known and frequently used surveyor in colonial Connecticut, and that his workmanship was accepted and desired by the authorities.

Chapter 8

A Lieutenant in King Philip's War

It has been said that it was necessary for every man on the Connecticut frontier to be available as a soldier. Except for public officials and ministers, every able bodied man between 16 and 60 was to be in the "traine band," as the local militia was then called. Thomas Leffingwell had been a soldier in the Pequot War, had lived with the Indians and spoke their language, and was an especially valued citizen soldier.

The Norwich militia, like the others, had a command structure of the ordinary soldiers at the bottom, then with increasing rank a corporal, a sergeant, an ensign, a lieutenant and a captain. Officers were confirmed by the General Court but were usually chosen by the local militia members. Leffingwell is known to have been a sergeant in October 1668 because he was identified as "Sargt Tho: Leffingwell" in the legislative records that month.[131] Rank in the militia was highly esteemed by the people, and gave titles for which men would forever afterward be called. Four years later in June 1672 the record shows that he was promoted with the entry that "This Court confirmes Mr. John Mason, Lieutenant, and Thomas Leffingwell, Ensigne, of the Traine Band of Norwich."[132] The local militias, of course, were composed of farmers and merchants of all ages, and were not professional soldiers. When called, however, they had a professional duty and job to do.

The legislature was constantly concerned with military preparedness in case of Indian uprising, so repeatedly encouraged the various militias of each town ("plantation") to have plenty of ammunition on hand. At the meeting starting on June 26, 1672, which Leffingwell attended, the legislature said that, "This Court upon speciall occasion have thought good and doe hereby order that the cheife military officers in each plantation doe forthwith take speciall care that the armes of their plantation and the severall soldiers thereof, be veiwed and set in sufficient repayre, well fixed and fitted for service; and that every person be furnished with amunition...."[133]

In a General Court review of militia strength, it was recorded that Norwich had seventeen men in the militia on August 11, 1673. This is a surprisingly low number, perhaps reflecting a period of inactivity of those who should have been enlisted. The legislature "ordered that each dragoone be provided with a good sword and belt, and serviceable muskett or kirbine, with a shott powch and powder and bulletts... and a horss to expedite their march."[134]

The concern about being prepared for war proved justified in 1675 when several Native American tribes in overwhelming numbers attacked English settlements throughout New England. It is sufficient to say that King Philip's War of 1675-1678 was incredibly deadly and terrifying. It was a shocking calamity to Puritan society. In proportion to population, the colonist death rate in New England in this conflict was far higher than both the Civil War and World War II were for the United States.[135]

More than half of the one hundred and ten English towns then existing were attacked, twelve of which were destroyed and many more damaged. The people were thrown into a terror, expecting to be attacked by Indians at any time without warning. It was the culmination of pent up Native American outrage for the loss of their lands and culture in New England. It will surprise no one to say that the Indians lost. In American history, outnumbered and with inferior weapons and supply, in the end they always lost. But in those early days of the war, the Native Americans did very well indeed, and inflicted an extremely painful revenge upon the English.

It may seem odd to learn that King Philip was not the ruler of England but was the chief of the Indians. That was the English name adopted by the sachem Metacom (sometimes called Metacomet), leader of the Wampanoag people. He was a patriot to his people and a scourge to his enemies. He rallied many tribes (not including Uncas and the Mohegans) to join his forces, and together they set New England on fire. In this war Indians killed settlers, the English killed Native Americans, and there was no limiting of the war to armies, warriors or soldiers.

In the winter of 1675 to 1676 the war was going very badly for the settlers in Massachusetts, and numerous towns were being destroyed and others abandoned. Fortunately for Thomas Leffingwell and his neighbors, most of the destruction fell on Massachusetts and Rhode Island and generally missed Connecticut. Nonetheless, Connecticut militias joined in the struggle and went to help the other colonies. Massachusetts had helped Connecticut in the Pequot War, and now that favor was returned. Settlers in Connecticut were fearful that their homes, farms and towns could be attacked at any time, and a constant watch was maintained.

With much to lose, the people of Norwich joined in the war effort. A company of men was organized in New London County, and Norwich contributed twenty men under Captain John Mason, Jr., and the newly promoted Lieutenant Thomas Leffingwell, with a number of Mohegans assisting them.[136]

English militiamen from Massachusetts, Connecticut and Rhode Island, along with Uncas and Mohegan warriors, struck against the Narragansett tribe on December 19, 1675. That tribe had so far not been in the fight. The battle was both a massacre of the Narragansetts and a disaster to the colonists. There is no doubt that Thomas Leffingwell was there.

Seventy-one Connecticut troops were killed in the battle, nine of which were from Captain John Mason Jr.'s Norwich men. The captain, who was the son of the famous John Mason who had commanded in the Pequot War, was grievously wounded. That would have left Lieutenant Leffingwell in command of the Norwich militia. Thomas Howard, one of the original founders of Norwich, was left dead on the battlefield. The wounded were brought home to Norwich, and the younger Captain Mason died from his wounds in his own house several months later. "This was emphatically the winter of gloom," wrote historian Caulkins.[137]

Decisions of war that could not wait for the next general meeting of the legislature were handled by a Council consisting of the Governor of the Colony, the Deputy Governor, and a few other men. That group considered various issues arising from the King Philips War on March 11, 1675/1676. "In regard of the present troubles that are upon us, and the heathen still continueing their hostility against the English and assaulting the plantations, to prevent their designs against us," the Council ordered that several steps be taken, including establishing diligent guarding of all towns to watch for attack. Also, men were urged to willingly join a nearby military force. "For the encouragement of such as shall goe forth [as] volunteers against our Indian enemies in the Narragansett Countrey... shall... goe forth under the command of Capt. George Denison... or Ens: Tho: Leffingwell, all such plunder as they shall sieze, to be divided amongst them."[138]

This order raises an uncomfortable aspect of the war, that soldiers in the King Philip's War were paid in part by the goods they could seize from the Indian villages and camps, which were pooled and then distributed equally among the individual soldiers to either keep or sell. The legislature did not have the money to pay soldiers, and this was a way to compensate the men for being away from their families and farms and risking death. Payment by "plunder" sounds harsh by today's standards and conjures up objectionable mental images, but this was the reality of the 1600s.

The man under whom Leffingwell served, Captain George Denison, was from New London, Connecticut, a few miles south of Norwich. Leffingwell already knew him as they had served together in the legislature. Denison was a veteran of war, having been a soldier in Oliver Cromwell's army in the English civil war, and with that experience had now been made a captain in King Philip's War. Thomas Leffingwell, a veteran of the Pequot War in the late 1630s, was the right person to serve and his second in command.

The location of Norwich on the northeastern frontier of Connecticut made it the most vulnerable town in the colony to attack, so this was the place where the New London County forces gathered. Other towns were ordered to send men to Norwich to form a permanent guard while the local men were away fighting. "The general court sent on from Hartford ten men, from New Haven eight, and from Fairfield eight, 'to lye in garrison at Norwich,' as a guard to the inhabitants. So great was the danger in those days, that the watch in each plantation was ordered, 'at least an hour before day, to call up the inhabitants, who should forthwith rise and arm themselves, march to the fort, and stand guard against any assault of the enemy until the sun be half an hour high in the morning.'"[139]

"The inhabitants of New London, Norwich, and Stonington," wrote 1600s Massachusetts historian William Hubbard, "apprehensive of their danger, by reason of the near bordering of the enemy... voluntarily [en]listed themselves" into military service under the local officers.[140] Captain Denison and Lieutenant Leffingwell commanded the men who had volunteered for military service, and Captain James Avery commanded the men who were drafted without having volunteered. The soldiers consisted of 42 volunteers, 37 drafted ("pressed") men, and about a hundred Native Americans fighting along with the English, mainly Mohegans and Pequots. There were, said historian Trumbull, "many inconveniences by this mixture of pressed men and volunteers."[141]

While the men were gathering at Norwich, just fifty miles to the east the war was going badly for the colonists. On March 26, 1676, sixty three English soldiers with about twenty friendly Indians were surrounded and massacred by some five hundred Narragansett warriors under Chief Canonchet near Providence, Rhode Island. Nine English survivors were captured and then tortured to death. Three days later the town of

Providence was burned.

The Connecticut soldiers had to act to protect their homes, and the expedition left Norwich on March 30, 1676. Five days later, on April 3rd, they captured an Indian woman. She told them that Chief Canonchet was in a nearby encampment with only thirty men, so Denison, Leffingwell and the others went in hot pursuit after him.

The running to ground of Canonchet by Denison and Leffingwell and their men was described as follows:

> Pushing rapidly onward, Denison's force spotted two warriors on the crest of a hill; pursuing them they came upon a small group of natives that fled in all directions. Canonchet, having no time to consult, and but little time to attempt an escape and no means to defend himself, bolted to the back side of the hill, throwing off his blanket, his silver-trimmed coat, and his belt of wampum. This only encouraged his pursuers, who suddenly realized they were closing in on the Narragansett sachem himself.
>
> Racing to the river, Canonchet waded in and slipped, falling into the water and soaking his gun. At this, his spirit seemed to dissolve...and he surrendered.[142]

The capture of Canonchet was a major event, one of the most important turning points of the war. Afterward the fortunes of the Native Americans declined and the security of the English settlers was enhanced. Thomas Leffingwell had now twice crossed the path of the Narragansetts. Once, years earlier, he had saved Uncas and the Mohegans when surrounded by the Narragansett under war chief Pessicus. Now, Leffingwell was closely involved in the capture of Chief Canonchet. "Captain Denison... returned to New London after an expedition into the Narragansett country, and reported that he had killed seventy-six hostiles."[143]

Chief Canonchet was turned over to colonial authorities, who offered him his life on the condition that he make peace with the English. He refused. When informed that he was to be put to death, he answered, "I like it well. I shall die before my heart is soft, and before I have spoken a word unworthy of myself."[144] He was afterward executed by the Mohegan Owaneco, a son of Uncas.

Through the remainder of the year 1676 the Connecticut and Indian forces under Major Talcott, Captain Denison and Lieutenant Leffingwell repeatedly raided the Narragansett country from their bases at Stonington and Norwich, going into Rhode Island and Massachusetts to find their enemies. Their ten or so back country expeditions over the following months disrupted Indian village life, farming, security, and morale, especially among the Narragansetts, and was in effect a guerrilla war against the Native Americans.

The soldiering done by Thomas Leffingwell and the men he served with had a significant impact on the war. One historian has noted that "the frequent raiding... prevented the Narragansetts from planting new fields and returning to caches of supplies, and the warriors from refitting for future battle in terms of weapons maintenance, ammunition acquisition and supply replenishment.... [T]he raids sunk and broke their spirits, and seems to have determined the fate of English and Indians, which until then was doubtful and uncertain."[145]

On May 10th Captain Denison brought much needed supplies to the Connecticut and Mohegan forces under Major Treat, the commander of all Connecticut forces. Leffingwell was not with them that day, as he had gone to Hartford to attend the legislature. The next morning he was present among the delegates of the General Court.

When the General Court met on May 11, 1676, King Philip's War was the cause of the greatest distress and concern among the legislators. "This Court haveing considered the present danger of the country by reason of the enemie's force and strength, and the outrages they committ upon the persons and estates of the good people of the United Colonyes, judg it necessary that there be forthwith raysed three hundred and fifty men in the Colony to be a standing army.... Each souldier to have a pownd of powder and three pownd of bulletts...." The troops were ordered to concentrate again at Norwich on May 27th. Numerous orders were issued for the supply, pay and other support of the military and the war in general. Men who lost horses and guns in the war were to be compensated.[146]

This Puritan legislature looked to the reason for the dreadful war, and found it to be caused, at least in part, to the lack of righteousness among the people. In the final analysis, it was the displeasure of God that brought this war upon them. The General Court, being both a civil and a religious body, reviewed the lifestyle of the citizens, and voted to remedy the personal and societal shortcomings that caused God to chastise them with this war.

These actions illustrates how the delegates, including Thomas Leffingwell who likely voted for these words, then viewed their world and their experiences. The legislature found that by various abuses the Sabbath "is prophaned..., which threatens the rooteing out of the power of godlyness and the procureing of the wrath and judgments of God upon us and our posteritie." Conducting sports or entertainment or drinking in public on Saturday night or Sunday were subjected to a fine of ten shillings. "It is allso farther ordered that noe... worke shall be done on the Sabboth... such as are not workes of piety, charaty or necessity, and no prophane discourse or talke, rude or unreverant behavioure shall be used on that holy day, upon the penalty of ten shillings fine."[147]

The Puritan delegates did not shrink from regulating personal conduct both in public and in private, even within the families and homes of the people. As reading the scriptures, teaching the gospel to children, holding daily prayer and giving thanks are "part of God's worship and the homage due to him," they were " to be atended conscientiously by every Christian famaly... Where any such neglect may be fownd, this Court doe solemnly recommend it to the ministry... to looke into the state of such famalyes, convince them of and instruct them in their duty." Town leaders were ordered to "inquire after such famalyes and assist the ministry for the reformation and education of the children in good litterature and the knowledge of the scripture according to good lawes allready provided. But if any heads... of such famalys shall be obstinate... and will not be reformed, that the grand jury present such persons to the county court, to be fined or punished or bownd to good behaviour, according to the demeritts of the case."

Travelers and visitors to the colony were to observe these religious duties along with the families with whom they were staying. Furthermore, stricter controls were placed on the serving of alcohol "in order to the preventing of the Increase of Drunckennesse. Upon complaynt of abuses that are groweing upon us by the retaylors of wines and liquors, this Court doe order that henceforth no person... shall retaile any less quantities then an anchor of drink at a time."

Except for the rich who were exempted, everyone else was restricted from wearing excessively fine clothing. "Whereas excess in apparell amongst us is unbecoming a wilderness condition and the profession of the gospell, whereby the riseing generation is in danger to be corrupted... It is therefore ordered by this Courte... that what person soever shall wear gold or silver lace, or gold or silver buttons, silk ribbons, or other superfluous trimings, or any bone lace above three shillings per yard, or silk scarfes" should be fined. "It is farther ordered that all such persons as shall... make or ware or buy any apparell exceding the quality and condition... that is apparently beyond the necessary end of apparell for covering or comelyness" should be fined.[148]

At the end of the General Court session, Leffingwell would have returned to his military duties, re-joining his militia in the field chasing hostile Indians. Although he is not specifically mentioned, he was likely present at the battle at the Pawtuxet River on July 2, 1676, seven miles from Providence, Rhode Island. Captain Denison was involved in it so it is very likely Leffingwell was there as well. War has excesses, and this one, like others, had cruelties and unnecessary killings. It was a massacre of about 170 Indian warriors, women, and children by the colonists. The next day the same thing happened to about 80 more Narragansetts waiting to surrender. The colonists viewed these events as destroying the Native American threat to the Connecticut settlements.

Metacomet, otherwise known as King Philip, was himself killed on August 12, 1676, at Bristol, Rhode Island. Ironically it was at the hand of another Indian on the side of the English. The war did not completely end then, as some Native Americans refused to surrender and carried on a resistance for a period of time.

As a result of these holdouts, the raids against the Indians continued. On Aug. 23, 1676, the Governor's Council issued the following order: "Whereas there are... some scattering parties of the enemies yet sculking in the woods, that may be dangerous at times... against the English, Captaine George Denison and Lnt. Tho: Leffingwell are therefore... commissioned and allowed to gather such volunteers as they shall prevayle withall to attend... to range the woods as they shall see cause and to kill and destroy, seize and surprize all such Indian enemies...."[149]

Lieutenant Thomas Leffingwell's participation in the war was extensive as both a soldier and a legislator. He lived with the uncertainty and fear that goes with war. What will happen, who will die, and who will be severely injured, is never known until the final shot has been fired. No doubt his family worried about him while he was gone, and he worried about his family that he left behind. Leffingwell was lucky. More than one thousand English colonists and three thousand Native Americans died in the war.

After the war the towns were rebuilt, new English settlers arrived, and life in the colonies went on. For the Indian tribes, many of their lands were permanently lost. There would never again be a serious and effective effort by the Indians to completely drive the English from New England. The English had won, and would never leave. Over time, King Philip's War has been almost entirely forgotten, but it was of the utmost seriousness for those who lived and died in it.

By the time the Connecticut colonial legislature assembled again in Hartford on October 12, 1676, the delegates were pleased that the war was effectively over. "This Court considering the enlarged goodness of God to his people in this wilderness, in appeareing so gloriously for their help in subdueing of our enemies in so good a measure as he hath done," it established another day of Thanksgiving to be observed on November first. It again called on the people, the towns, and the local churches to encourage and enforce righteous living "to seek the presence and blessing of the Lord upon his people... and that he would appear for the help and salvation of his people in this wilderness...."[150]

After the return of peace, Thomas Leffingwell placed a priority on gaining compensation for the ordinary soldiers of King Philip's War with grants of land. He had likely received real property for his service in the Pequot War, which had gotten him on his way to becoming a prosperous Freeman, and he wanted others to receive the same opportunity. In October 1696 legislative records stated that "Liet. Thomas Leffingwell of Norwich and Sergt. John Frink of Stonington moved this Court that they with the rest of the English volunteers in the former wars might have a plantation granted to them. This Court grants them a tract of land six miles square for a plantation, to be taken up out of some of the conquered land" from the Narragansetts.[151] This area was surveyed and settled, and became the community of Voluntown, Connecticut.

Ownership of the land was conveyed to a committee of seven men, including Leffingwell, which was to oversee the distribution to the former soldiers. In 1701 a list of the names of the volunteers was put together, and Leffingwell was appointed as part of the team to decide the correctness of the claims of service made by the various men. There were about 180 claims made. Lots were chosen and the land was divided. Thomas Leffingwell received his recompense for service in the war along with the others.[152]

This historical marker is at the main crossroads in Voluntown, Connecticut. Thomas Leffingwell's role in establishing the community is memorialized.

Chapter 9

A Witness to Saving the Colonial Charter

After the King Philip's War Thomas Leffingwell continued the life he had lived before. He continued to be a family man, worked his farm in Norwich, did survey work for cash, dealt in lands as opportunities came, and served in the colonial legislature of Connecticut. He continued to be in the Norwich militia, with the General Court in May 1780 confirming " "Mr. James Fitch... [as] Captain of Norwich traine band, and Thomas Leffingwell Lnt....of said Traine band."[153]

As the years continued to pass, Leffingwell's life revolved around his family, the addition of more grandchildren every year, the growing of crops, maintaining the farm and animals, social relations with neighbors and friends, and the observance of the Puritan religion. It's unfortunate that more details of these aspects of his life are not available. Instead, there is information about his service in the legislature. It must be remembered that important though it was, the legislature was only one facet of his life and not the central part of it. Yet it does in some insightful ways reveal the man, Thomas Leffingwell.

Although votes for and against particular actions are not recorded, it is reasonable to assume that Thomas Leffingwell supported most and perhaps all of the actions taken by the General Court. It can be considered that whatever the legislature did and said generally reflected the views and beliefs of Leffingwell personally. Also, these actions illustrate the nature of Thomas Leffingwell's life and world in the 1600s.

When he attended the session of the General Court starting May 10, 1677, Leffingwell was part of the decision to give relief to the people who owed money but had their farms and lives disrupted by the war. "This Court by reason of the late troubles of the warr and the incumbrances thereof," the record states, "doe see good reason to grant liberty of one yeare more from the first of June next for creditors to make up their accounts with their debtors...."[154] Whatever debts were due, the people had an extension of one more year to pay them.

Leffingwell took a break from public service for most of the next four years, tending to his own needs and business. Between October of 1677 and May of 1681 he served in only one session of the legislature. He was back on October 13, 1681, and was elected to most of the sessions thereafter. He was an ongoing presence as the legislators gathered for each session.

When he returned to his seat in the Hartford assemblage, he and the other delegates dealt with neighboring colonies almost like Connecticut was an independent country. In May 1682 they responded frostily when New York colonists settled on land claimed by Connecticut. "This Court being informed that some people of New Yorke have setled within the limits of this colony, on the east side of Hudson's River, doe order a letter be sent in the name of this Court to the Governor of New Yorke to signify our dislike of their so intrenching upon our charter limits," the legislature said, "and... that they should remove themselves off our lands speedily...."[155]

The legislature in October 1682 appointed Thomas Leffingwell and Captain James Avery to be arbitrators in a dispute between two individuals. John Wheeler and Lawrence Codner "doe referre the issue and determination of all such differences... [and]... "doe bind themselves to stand to and abide by and fulfill... whatsoever they shall return as their issue [decision]...."[156] Presumably, the matter was heard, the decision was rendered by Leffingwell and Avery, and it was accepted.

Some things never change, and ancient problems persist today. The General Court session in October 1684 took up the issue of the bad roads throughout Connecticut. "Whereas there is a great neglect fownd in mayntaining of the high wayes between towne and towne, the wayes being incumbred with dirty slowes [swamps], bushes, trees and stones &c., this Court doe therefore order that each plantation [town]... shall forthwith take sufficient care that the highwayes... be well amended from such defects and so kept from time to time. The survayours of each towne to see this attended, according to law..."[157]

Leffingwell was present when the legislature in May 1686 passed an "An Act for preventing of fraud concerning Horses." It provided that notwithstanding all efforts to prevent "deceit and evill dealing which hath been used in takeing up, marking and conveying away of horses... out of this colony, to the great loss and damage of the inhabitants, and for that as yet the evill is not suppressed." The Court therefore ordered a number of remedies, including an order "that each towne shall appoynt one brander or more... [to] make and keep a true record of all such horss kind which shall be presented to them, of the person clayming, and naturall and artificiall marks and the age and colour as neer as they may, entering the same in one booke in each plantation, and shall affix the towne brand upon every such beast which shall be... presented to him...."[158]

He was also present in May 1693 when the General Court dealt with trespassing on land, and using it as a path of travel without the permission of the owner. "Severall complaynts being made by many of the inhabitants of this Colony of the great wrong don in many places and to many persons by frequent passing... over cornfeilds or grass land where ther is no alowed way, to the great damage and provocation of the proprietors of sayd lands, ...this Court doe therefore enact that whosoever shall be found passing over any mans inclosed land... without the proprietors leave... where there is no allowed highway... every such person so offending shall forfeit to the owners... one shilling if he be on foote and two shilling and six pence if he be on horsback...."[159]

A Homeland for the Eastern Pequot Tribe

Thomas Leffingwell was one of the principal men involved in the establishment of a permanent and protected tribal home for the Pequots under Chief Mamoho in 1683. The colonial legislature was much aware of Leffingwell's history of good relations with the Native Americans and his speaking of their language, so he was well suited to help them. Since the Indians had confidence in the man, they would be more likely to accept what he recommended.

By the early 1680s Chief Mamoho and his small Pequot tribe were in a destitute condition and without a legally protected homeland. The tribe had been very nearly exterminated in the Pequot War in the 1630s, and afterward was mostly taken over by Uncas and the Mohegans. Yet a small band survived as their own people, and they petitioned the colonial Connecticut legislature to provide them some land as a place to live, hunt, and farm.

At the session convening on May 10, 1683 the issue came before the delegates, and they took action to help the tribe. "This Court doth appoynt Captn James Fitch, Captn James Avery and Lnt Tho. Leffingwell to be a committee in behalfe of this Court to move the people of Stoneington to lay out to the Pequots under Mawmohoe's goverment a suitable tract of land that may be sufficient for them to plant upon." Leffingwell and the others were "ordered to use utmost endeavoures to suit them with a sufficient tract of land...." If all else failed, they should give them some unimproved property in Stonington under "the law requireing every towne to provide for their own Indians."

Leffingwell, Fitch and Avery did in fact find a home for the Indians. The land on Lantern Hill in Stonington, where the Pequots were already located, was claimed by a farmer named Isaac Wheeler. Leffingwell, Fitch and Avery convinced Wheeler to release his claim in exchange for other land elsewhere that was owned by the colonial government. "The 'utmost endeavors' of this committee were crowned with success," the record stated in the 1850s, "and the miserable remnant of the Pequots and eastern Nianticks, under Mamoho's government, at last found a resting place."[160] After securing this 280 acres of land for the Indians, the legislature appointed Leffingwell with two others to survey it and record it to prevent further encroachment by English settlers.[161] Because of the work done by Leffingwell and the committee, this beautiful land has been, and still is, the home of the Eastern Pequot Tribal Nation.

The Connecticut Colonial Charter Crisis

As a delegate to the legislature of the colony, Thomas Leffingwell witnessed and was a part of a famous incident in Connecticut history. He was present when the government was usurped by the King's representative, Edmund Andros, and the colonial charter was hidden in a tree.

Colonial Connecticut was a part of the British Empire, and although very remote from national events in London, it nonetheless was very much affected by what went on there. In 1662 King Charles II granted a charter to the colony of Connecticut in which "all the king's subjects in the colony should enjoy all the privileges of free and natural subjects within the realm of England." It established a government with a governor, and a legislature (General Court) selected by the local people.[162] King Charles also was tolerant of the Church of England, dissenters from that church, and Catholics. The Puritans of New England were dissenters within the Church of England, and appreciated his broad view of religion as a national policy, though they did not share that tolerance with others at the local level.

Life went along happily in Connecticut under these circumstances, but not so happily in England. The 1600s were years of struggle in Britain, as civil wars raged, religions sought to suppress each other, and parliament challenged the king for political power. There was an unsuccessful conspiracy to overthrow King Charles, and the blame for it fell upon the dissenters from the Church of England. That included the Puritans over in the colonies.

The local officials in Connecticut were worried, fearing that the liberties they enjoyed might be ended by an angry monarch. On November 14, 1683, a special session of the General Court was held to help make amends with the King and avert any retribution that might come their way, such as revocation of the colonial charter. Thomas Leffingwell was present at this urgent meeting, and undoubtedly joined in approving the letter that was sent to King Charles II:

> To the High and Mighty Charles the 2d... - The most humble Petition of your Majestie's loyall subjects, The Governor and Generall Assembly of his Majestie's Colony of Conecticutt in New England, humbly sheweth:
>
> Most dread Soveraigne, We humbly beseech your Majestie to cast a favourable aspect upon us and to take notice... of our loyall affections towards your Majestie, although they come from us not trimmed with quaintness of language, but in a plaine habbit, according to the manor of a poore wildernesse people whoe studdy realities and not flatteries: and in the words of truth and sobernesse, as becometh loyall subjects, we have sayd, we doe and will say, God save the King....
>
> And whereas we have... been informed of some horible

complotments against your Majestie's person... we doe abhorr and detest the same, and shall make it manifest by our words and workes, prayers and practices, that we are men of other principles, and doe heartily return thankes to Almighty God for the preservation he hath granted your Majestie's and Goverment...

Most dread Soveraigne, we humbly pray the continuance of your grace and favour, in the full injoyment of those former priviledges and liberties you have out of your princely grace and bounty bestowed upon us in your Royall Charter granted this corporation....

The Governor and Generall Assembly of your Majestie's Colony of Connecticut, Hartford, November 14th, 1683. Robert Treat, Governor.[163]

To modern people not living in a monarchy, this letter seems overly submissive. But Thomas Leffingwell and the other delegates were men of the 1600s who did what they must to preserve their freedoms. The results of their efforts succeeded temporarily. When the Massachusetts Bay Colony charter was revoked several months later, the same fate did not befall Connecticut.

In February of 1685 King Charles II died unexpectedly, and he was succeeded at the throne by his brother, James II. There was considerable anxiety that this new King would revoke the charter and the political rights of Connecticut, and Leffingwell was present on May 14, 1685, when the Governor and General Court sent James II a letter:

We humbly beg the continuance of your Majesties favoure and clemency towards us, that we, under your Majesties protection, may be made happy in the injoyment of our proprietors and priviledges conferd upon us by our late Soveraigne your Majestie's most dear brother.

Gracious Sir, We shall not cease to lift up our hearts to allmighty God to bless your Majestie with a long and happy reign, that we may continue a happy people, under the Goverment of so gracious a Prince, in these remoat parts of America ; who have taken the first opportunety humbly to present ourselves before your Majestie with our most sincere promises of all fayth and allegiance.... [164]

These supplications and professions of loyalty did not work. King James II wanted to eliminate the multiple colonial governments and their charters and establish a single Dominion of New England. The Dominion would include New Jersey, New York, Connecticut, Rhode Island, Massachusetts, New Hampshire, and Maine, with a single governor appointed by the King.

The charter of 1662 was to be revoked and Connecticut was to be abolished. Thomas Leffingwell was at the meeting of the General Council on October 31, 1687, when Sir Edmond Andros, the King's Governor of the Dominion of New England, came to end the separate political existence of the colony of Connecticut.

The legend is that during this meeting Governor Andros demanded the surrender of the actual paper that was the charter of Connecticut, which was laid out before them on a table. Suddenly the candles were blown out, there was a flurry of activity in the darkness, and when light and order were restored, the charter was gone. It was claimed that some of the delegates had taken the document and hidden it in the hollow of an oak tree. That tree was forever after known as the "charter oak."[d] The name "charter oak" has become part of the founding mythology of Connecticut, taught in every class of state history, and is the name of a great many businesses, health clinics, land developments, companies, a college, and even a cigar.

There is a less dramatic theory of the incident. It is that the original charter document was withheld and hidden from Governor Andros, and he left with a mere copy of it.

On that occasion, whatever actually occurred, Thomas Leffingwell was present in the room with Governor Andros, the other delegates, and the charter. The official record of the meeting stated simply that "His Excelency Sr Edmond Andross... by order from his Majestie James the second... took into his hands the Government of this colony of Connecticott, it being by his Majestie annexed to the Massachusetts & other colonys under his

---

[d]Offshoots from the charter oak tree were later transplanted to many towns around the state. The tree was blown down in a storm in 1856, but wood salvaged from it was made into a chair now displayed in the Hartford Capitol Building.

Excelencies Government. Finis."[165]

"Finis" was an apt word to describe the way the people viewed this development. The government of Connecticut was finished; it was the end. Thomas Leffingwell, like the other delegates, surely went home discouraged and angry. What was to become of Connecticut, where he had invested the last fifty years of his life?

"King James the second began his reign in the most flagrant violation of the laws," recorded historian Benjamin Trumbull in the 1790s. "His reign grew more intolerable from year to year until he became the general abhorrence of the nation. He proceeded in the same lawless and cruel manner with the colonies, vacating their charters, and governing them by the worse measures and the worst men."[166] The King's Governor of New England, Edmond Andros, ended colonial self-government and its elective offices, imposed taxes at will, and assessed high fees for governmental services. The Puritans were outraged when he ended government support of churches.

Fortunately for the people of Connecticut, the reign of King James II was short-lived, and was overthrown in England by November of 1688. This event became known in British history as "the Glorious Revolution." William of Orange, a Protestant, was made the new king. When word reached Boston, Governor Andros was arrested by the local population. The Dominion of New Englad was ended, and the several colonies were restored to their separate identities.

After a year and a half of suspension, the Connecticut General Court, including Thomas Leffingwell, joyfully met again in Hartford on May 9, 1689. The government of Connecticut was reestablished. "Whereas this Court hath been interupted in the management of the Government in this Colony of Conecticutt, for neer eighteen months past, and our lawes and courts have been disused...," the legislature announced, "It is now enacted, ordered and declared, that all the lawes of this Colony formerly made, according to Charter, and courts constituted in this Collony for administration of justice, as they were before the late interruption, shall be of full force and vertue for the future... according to charter."[167] The status quo existing before King James II and Governor Andros was re-established.

Just as Thomas Leffingwell and most of the people had hoped, the restored colonial charter of Connecticut was indeed saved, and did in fact govern the colony for more than a hundred years.

Final Years in the Colonial Legislature

The colonial legislature and Thomas Leffingwell's role in it resumed as it was before the political interruption. Local matters within the colony came back into view.

Puritans wanted everyone to learn to read and write to be better people in general, but also so that they could study the Bible for themselves. Leffingwell was present for the passage of two measures on education. The legislature found "that notwithstanding the former orders made for the education of children and servants, there are many persons unable to read the English tongue, and thereby uncapeable to read the holy word of God, or the good lawes of the Colony...." To remedy this, "it is hereby ordered that all parents and masters shall cause theire respective children and servants, as they are capeable, to be taught to read distinctly the English tongue...." Also, "considering the necessity and great advantage of good literature," the delegates "doe order and appoynt that there shall be two free schooles kept and mayntayned in this Colony, for the teaching of all such children as shall com there, after they can first read the psalter, to teach such reading, writeing, arithmetick, the Lattin and Greek tongues..." One school was to be at Hartford, and the other at New Haven....[168]

At the General Court session in October 1693 Thomas Leffingwell was present to vote in favor of the salary paid the delegates for their attendance. "Court grants the Deputies of the Court two shillings six pence per day for their attendance at Court from this day."[169] This was his own daily compensation.

It is noteworthy that at the May 9, 1700, session the General Court "doth appoint Lieut. Thomas Leffingwell and Mr. Jonath. Tracye to lay out lands formerly granted by the Generall Court to Mr. Anthonie Howkins according to the tenor of said grant."[170] This had happened many times before, but by now Leffingwell was seventy-six years old. He must have been in good enough health and fitness to do this job, ride a horse, hike through the hills, woods, and undergrowth and see well enough to survey the land.

When the legislature of the colony of Connecticut gathered on October 10, 1700, it was the 53rd and final session for Thomas Leffingwell. At this last meeting he was still advancing the interests of the veterans of the King Philip's War. "Lieut. Thomas Leffingwell [and others] in behalfe of the rest of the volunteers, moved this Assembly for a confirmation of the said tract of land to the said volunteers for their use...." The request for the land at

Voluntown to be given to the war veterans was granted by the General Court, and the long public service of Thomas Leffingwell to the citizens of Norwich and Connecticut came to an end.[171]

In May of 1701 the son of Thomas Leffingwell, Thomas 2d, was appointed as Ensign of the militia at Norwich.[172] Thereafter, father and son were distinguished by their rank, with Lieutenant Thomas Leffingwell being the father, and Ensign Thomas Leffingwell the son.

Thomas Leffingwell the younger, designated as Ensign in the record, served in the General Court on May 13, 1703. At that session the legislature voted to create "a township... called by the name of Windham... and that... [Lieutenant] Thomas Leffingwell [and several other men]... [were] the proprietors thereof."[173] This founding of the town of Windham was another of Thomas Leffingwell's final public acts. The elder Leffingwell was one of the founding group of proprietors of Windham, and he with Richard Bushnell and Simon Huntington made the original survey of the town.

Service in Norwich

Throughout these years, Leffingwell also did public service in his home town of Norwich. There was no separation of church and state in Connecticut, and no effort or even thought to move in that direction. The people were a political body that handled all matters of the community, whether religious or secular. The people built a meeting hall that served both church and state, for Sabbath services on Sunday and for town government meetings on other days.

On May 20, 1689, the town council appointed Leffingwell and a couple of others to put into effect the decision to enlarge the meeting house.[174] On December 21, 1691, Leffingwell was elected Townsman, serving along with three others. He served in that capacity for much of the 1690s and the year 1700. On March 8, 1693/1694 he was appointed to do a survey for the town, something that would happen often, as it had with the colonial legislature.

The inhabitants in 1694 recognized that they had not kept very good records of the first settlement of Norwich thirty years earlier, and appointed a committee "to search out and do the best they can," to find the names of the original settlers and to identify the land each one had been granted. Some of the surviving original settlers were named as participants, including Thomas Leffingwell and Thomas Adgate (the step-father of Leffingwell's daughter-in-law Mary Bushnell Leffingwell and son-in-law Joseph Bushnell).[175] By now Leffingwell was in his early 70s, and one of the aging but venerable Norwich founders, a dwindling group as the years passed.

In 1694 the Reverend James Fitch, who had served the people as church pastor for forty years in both Saybrook and in Norwich, was felled by a disabling stroke. It was plain to the town leaders that another minister was needed. In a curiously worded resolution they decided to get an additional clergyman to assist the ailing Fitch. "Inasmuch as it hath pleased God to lay his afflicting hand upon our Reverend Pastor Mr. James Fitch that at present he is disabled with respect to the work of the ministry among us," it said, "Wherefore, the towne appoint Left. Thomas Leffingwell [and others as] a committee to treat with Mr. Jabez Fitch with respect unto his succeeding of his father in the work of the ministry among us."[176] The son, a recent graduate of Cambridge, came for a year as a trial run of being the minister. At the end of that year Leffingwell was appointed again to work with him about staying permanently, but the young man declined. Leffingwell and the other committee members continued their search for years before a permanent minister was found.

Class distinction was recognized and important in 1600s society, even in church. There was a square pew in which the first rank of people were seated to hear from the minister, with others seated in declining order of social status.[177] On March 28, 1698, the church appointed five of the venerable older men in town, including Thomas Leffingwell, "to seat the inhabitants in the meeting house" for Sabbath services "with due regard to rank." This perceived need to seat people according to their station in society was an unfortunate one, and caused problems in the community. "Frequent disputes and even long-continued feuds were caused by this perplexing business of seating a congregation according to rank and dignity," wrote local historian Frances Caulkins.[178] Just where Thomas and Mary Leffingwell sat in this ranking of the people is not known.

Chapter 10

A Royal Commissioner
in the Mohegan Land Case

The Mohegans, although never at war with the English, and in fact their positive allies in times of great need - such as in the Pequot War and King Philip's War- nevertheless lost their lands to the European settlers. In this respect, in the end they fared no better as friends than other tribes did as enemies. Too generously, Chief Uncas had over the years deeded away some of his people's earthly domain, but always maintained a home ground for the tribe. His sons, however, had no such restraints. It seems fair to say that they knew not what they did. None of them had a complete understanding of the English common law concept of private land ownership, and its exclusive and perpetual nature.

With the advance of age, Uncas was no longer the man and leader he had once been, and he lost control of events. Owaneco, his son, battled alcohol, and admitted that his numerous land grants were given to settlers "taking advantage of me, when I am in drink."[179] The English were all too willing to accept his foolish offerings. In an incident in 1704 a drunken Owaneco fell out of a canoe, and the Englishmen who saved him from drowning were each deeded one hundred acres in gratitude.[180] This over-generosity made it impossible to keep a sizeable Mohegan homeland.

In the early 1680s, Uncas, now well past eighty years in age, became very concerned about the future of his people, where they would live, and how they would maintain themselves. He began a concerted effort to save what land the Mohegans still had and to regain whatever he could. It was his final effort as chief. As was recorded in the records of the colonial legislature, Uncas said that he knew "not how long he shall live and how soon he may dye, and is desireous to leave peace twixt his children & people and the English."[181] Thomas Leffingwell would become involved in many of the responses of the colonists to the various requests of Uncas, at town, colony and royal levels.

Uncas was concerned about three particular issues with Norwich, and approached the town about them. Thomas Leffingwell was appointed to a town committee to work with him in finding solutions. Leffingwell's presence is clearly seen in the kindly attitude and sentimental words of their September 1682 agreement.[182]

First, there was a "small Tract of Land" that Uncas especially wanted for his people along the boundary between Norwich and the homeland that was called "Mohegan." Leffingwell and his fellow citizens wanted to simply give it to him, without worrying about whether his claim was just or not:

> This Town, considering... him as an Old Friend, see cause to gratify him with the said land as a gift to him and his heirs forever.

Second, Uncas claimed that three pounds in money were due for the purchase of the town. Leffingwell and the town people did not see a basis for this, but again they wanted to accommodate the aging chief:

> Though there is nothing appearing how the money is due...yet notwithstanding the Town have granted his desire as not willing to dissatiefie an old friend in such a small matter.

Lastly, Uncas wanted his people to be able in the future to fish the river, and the town again demonstrated their high regard for him:

> We also satisfie him in this writing about it, that he and his successors shall from time to time, and at all times, have full and free liberty to make use of the rivers and ponds.

Uncas, the document declared, was "fully satisfied" with the agreement. The old sachem made his famous insignia, known as "the mark of Uncas," and then it was signed by Thomas Leffingwell. Below his name were the signatures of the other members of the town committee.[183]

This is a remarkable document. The hand and heart of Thomas Leffingwell can be felt behind it. The three requests were each granted. It shows in written form the genuine personal affection and regard between Thomas Leffingwell and Chief Uncas, and between the people of Norwich and the Mohegan sachem. Much of the English and American treatment of Native Americans is regrettable and reprehensible, but here is a small but bright light in the relationships among individuals and peoples.

Uncas could not write in English lettering and so used a mark
of his own design, which varied somewhat on each document.
This is a facsimile of his mark on the 1682 agreement with
Thomas Leffingwell and the town of Norwich. (William L. Stone, Uncas
and Miantonomoh: A Historical Discourse, published 1842, p. 202.)

About a year later, some time in the fall of 1683, Uncas died. It is nowhere recorded, but it seems likely, that Thomas Leffingwell went south of town and paid his old friend a final visit. Leffingwell lived true to the spirit of their life-long friendship, not only while Uncas lived but also afterward. More than twenty years later, as a Royal Commissioner appointed by Queen Anne, he would again raise his voice to support the land claims of Uncas and of the Mohegan people for a tribal homeland.

Prior to his death Uncas had approached the Connecticut General Court and asked that his lands be specifically identified and protected. Five years later, in May 1685, there were issues about the exact location of the Mohegan boundaries with Norwich on the north and with New London on the south. The legislature did "appoynt... Lnt. Tho. Leffingwell [and four others]... to lay out the line between New London and Mohegans, and between Norwich and the Indians, and make return thereof that it may be entered on record in October."[184] At that same session, when considering the Mohegan claims to the lands of the Wabaquasset tribe, Leffingwell and two other delegates "are by this Court desired and appoynted to hear what the Indians have to say in theire cases, and to prepare their matters for the Court's determination."[185]

With Leffingwell's friendly relationship with the Mohegans and their respect for and trust in him, his presence in the surveying of boundaries and listening to grievances was a calming and steadying influence. In fact, Thomas Leffingwell believed that the Mohegan people had been wrongfully dispossessed of some of their lands, and that the lands in question should be restored to the tribe.

Others, including the colonial Governor of Connecticut and landowners encroaching on historic Indians lands, did not look so favorably upon the claims of Uncas. Beginning in 1687 the colony began granting lands to settlers that had previously been considered to be Mohegan. John Mason's family, ever the friend and protector of the tribe, in 1704 petitioned Queen Anne to have it stopped and reversed. In an effort to untangle the conflicting assertions, she authorized a Royal Commission in inquire into what became known as the "Mohegan Land Claim."

By this time Thomas Leffingwell was eighty years old. "And now we come to our last glimpse of him as one of Her Majesty's Commissioners," wrote Dr. Albert Leffingwell in 1897. The official record established his appointment in these words: "Whereas, Her Majesty, Queen Anne, by her Majesty's Commission, under the Great Seal of England, bearing date the 19th day of July, 1704,.. did authorize and appoint Joseph Dudley Esq. then Her Majesty's Captain-General and Governor of the Province of Massachusetts, in New England,... Thomas Leffingwell of Norwich, in Connecticut, [and others]... to be Commissioners,... *Commanding them*, after having heard both parties, to determine according to Justice and Equity, and *to restore said [Mohegan] Indians to their settlements, in case they had been unjustly dispossessed....*"[186] [Emphasis added.]

Pursuant to this empowerment, the Royal Commission held a hearing in Stonington, Connecticut, on August 23, 1705. When he went to Stonington for the commission business, Leffingwell may well have stayed in the home of his oldest daughter, Rachel. She had married Robert Parke of Stonington, and still lived there with her large brood of children.

Writs had been previously issued, summoning the governor and colonial government, the white claimants of the lands in controversy, the Mohegan tribe, and all parties concerned, to attend a hearing at that time and place. The court consisted of Joseph Dudley, Edward Palmes, Giles Sylvester, Jr., Jahleel Brenton, Nathaniel Byfield, Thomas Hooker, James Avery, John Avery, John Morgan, and Thomas Leffingwell.[187] They were collectively known as "the Dudley Commission."

This was a significant group of men, both in government position and in family connections. Dudley was the Governor of Massachusetts and president of the Commission. Palmes lived in New London and was the son-in-law of Governor Winthrop of Connecticut. Brenton was the son of Governor William Brenton of Rhode Island. Sylvester was from New Haven, Connecticut. Byfield was a prominent judge in Rhode Island. Hooker was the son of one of the prime founders of Connecticut, who was also named Thomas Hooker. Morgan had been a captain in King Philip's War, lived in Preston, Connecticut, and had been a delegate to the colonial legislature. Leffingwell was well acquainted with James Avery, who had been his companion in King Philip's War and in the colonial legislature. They also served together on the committee appointed to find a home for Chief Mamoho and the Eastern Pequots twenty years earlier.

The Royal Commission hearing was held on August 23, 1705. The parties were each given the opportunity to present their case on the ownership of the lands in question, whether they be Mohegan or English It quickly degenerated into a judicial nightmare, becoming a swamp of legal maneuvering. The attorneys for the colonial government and for the English landowner claimants said that they had just now learned that the Commission intended to actually decide the matter itself and not merely gather information for the Queen's government. They declared they would not participate because the Commission was exceeding its authority.

They were wrong on this point because the charge from London commanded the Commission "to restore said [Mohegan] Indians to their settlements, in case they had been unjustly dispossessed...."[188] Nevertheless, the attorneys for the Connecticut colonial government and for the landowner were hostile and disrespectful in their demeanor. As the record of proceedings stated, the attorneys...

> ...drew up to Col. Dudley and told him they were come to read a paper to him. [H]e told them the Commissioners were just sitting down, and when the Court was opened, they should be heard; they insist upon it to read it presently, and he refused it and proceeded to open the Court. The Sheriff of the County came up to us [the Commissioners] and commanded silence in a very imperious manner, and the Gentlemen went on to read their paper, and then laid it down on the Board and drew off a very little distance, but within hearing of the Court, and then proceeded again to command silence and read publicly a protestation against the Court, and then returned several times in a very insolent manner while the Court was publicly proceeding in reading papers and hearing the complaint. Col. Dudley prayed them to be patient, they should be heard in their turn. Whiting told him boldly they had no business, and Chester they would

not be put upon, and Saltonstall, one of the persons complained of for entering on the Indian lands, said the Commissioners were no Court, and that Her Majesty's commands contradict one another, and that he was forbidden to answer by the Government... [O]ne of their Ministers present when... [a witness was being sworn in], drew him back by the sleeve to hinder his oath.

The colonial attorneys then walked out the door and refused to participate further. It seems likely that the government's lawyers realized they would lose the case on the merits, the facts and the law, and so raised a technical issue to attempt to sink the proceedings.

The Royal Commissioners, however, would not be sunk. They proceeded with the hearing and called for the attorneys for the Mohegans and the Mason family to present their case. This they did. Afterward, no representative of the Governor or the English claimants was in attendance to rebut the Mohegan evidence or offer a contrary argument.

In addition, the members of the Commission themselves had information that they personally knew of the situation, and they gave their own testimony as well. To modern legal standards, judges giving evidence may seem inappropriate, but this was more than three hundred years ago when the law was different, perhaps in some ways better. The Queen had instructed the Commission to look into the Mohegan land claims and appointed members with extensive personal information concerning the facts, so using their knowledge seems far more logical than ignoring it.

According to Norwich historian Frances Caulkins, Thomas Leffingwell testified of his long relationship with the Mohegans, saying that he had personally known Uncas since the year 1637, and that Uncas had always assisted the English.[189] Leffingwell was "a tried friend of the Indians, and from his intimate acquaintance with the affairs of the tribe, he had great influence" with the other Royal Commissioners.[e] His decision, she said, was theirs.[190]

---

[e]The documents concerning Leffingwell's comments were available to Frances Caulkins in the 1860s but are not to be found today. Hopefully, they exist somewhere in a private collection and will some day come to light.

After due deliberation the Royal Commissioners ruled in favor of the Mohegan claims and against the colony of Connecticut and the encroaching Englishmen. In their written judgment they said that, "We are... unanimous in our opinion, that Uncas and Owaneko are the only steady Sachims in this Province to the English interest, in all times without the least challenge; that the Indians of his Tribe have marched at all times in the service of the English, and bin very successful in these 70 years past...." The Commissioners went on to issue several findings, each of which stated the opinions and conclusions of Thomas Leffingwell:

(1) that Owaneco is the true Sachem of the Mohegan Indians

(2) That he and his ancestors have always been loyal to...England

(3) and that the Government of Connecticut have by several treaties acknowledged them to have lands of their own.

(4) The Mohegan Indians had an undoubted right to a very large tract of land within that Colony, lying to E. of Connecticut River, and the English inhabitants of New London, Norwich, Stonington and others have acknowledged their right to those lands....

(9) Contrary to these reservations and treaties, the Government of Connecticut have granted away considerable tracts of the planting grounds of the Mohegans amounting to about 3,000 acres....

(10) The Mohegans have been very unjustly turned out of planting ground called Massapeage, lying within the township of New London, the improvement of which land is reserved to them by their deed to New London. (

(11) The town of Lyme, under pretence of their grant of their township from the Colony have taken into their improvement that tract of the Mohegan lands... about 9 miles by 2.

(12) One other very large tract of their hunting ground is granted away from the Mohegans to the township of Colchester, viz. between Norwich, Haddam, Lyme, Lebanon and Mattabesset.

(13) The Mohegans are a considerable tribe, consisting of 150 fighting men, formerly a much greater number, and cannot subsist without their lands. They have been extremely grieved at these proceedings and have

frequently applied to the General Assembly for redress, but could obtain none, whereby they have been reduced to great want and necessity, and are in great danger of deserting their ancient friendship.

The Court are unanimously of the opinion that they [the Mohegans] ought to be restored to the said lands enumerated, and that... the Government of Connecticut be required immediately to cause them to be so restored....[191] [Emphasis added.]

The judgment of the Royal Commission was signed first by Governor Dudley and then by each one of the Commissioners. This included Thomas Leffingwell, who had come again in an effort to rescue the Mohegans.

The Royal Commission judgment was immediately challenged. The colonial government appealed the decision and the litigation went on for decades. Outside of Norwich, the opposition to the judgment was extreme. The attorneys for the Connecticut government heatedly argued that the decision by Leffingwell and the others "was carried wholly by intrigue and the grossest misrepresentations. The commission was granted by her majesty, wholly upon an ex parte hearing, upon the representation of the enemies of the colony; and the men who carried on the intrigue, were appointed judges in their own case. Without hearing the case, contrary to all reason and justice, they gave judgment against the colony, and hundreds of individuals." The colonial officials were treated, the lawyers said, "with dishonour and contempt."[192]

The heat of the opposition is evident. Such venomous accusations in colonial government circles to a man who had served in fifty-three sessions of the legislature must have been personally disconcerting to Thomas Leffingwell, even though he was completely comfortable with the decision he had made.

The rights which Leffingwell and his fellow Commissioners had recognized in favor of the Mohegans in 1705 were never enforced by the English or Connecticut governments. While in England in the 1730s trying to gain an audience with the King, Mohegan Chief Mahomet Weyonomon, great-grandson of Uncas, died in London, still waiting for the King, and unheard.

When the case was finally and permanently decided in London courts in 1767, the Mohegan rights were lost. No one with personal knowledge of the facts was still alive. Norwich historian Frances Caulkins wrote a hundred years later that, "It was the prevalent opinion in England that the Mohegans had right on their side, but that it was not expedient to do them justice."[193]

Sixty years earlier, however, Thomas Leffingwell, had found it expedient to do justice to the Mohegans. And he did.

Chapter 11

Avoiding Probate

Living on the southeast corner of the intersection of two country roads, now called Washington Street and Harland Road in Norwich, Thomas Leffingwell enjoyed life as a venerated senior of the community. He had been on the Connecticut frontier seventy years earlier, and an early settler of Saybrook and a co-founder of Norwich. He knew many people, and everyone knew him.

Even without any supporting evidence, there is no doubt that after 1700 Thomas Leffingwell, now in his eighties, spent a great deal of time across the street in the tavern owned and run by his son, Ensign Thomas Leffingwell. He would have been good company then, hanging out at the tavern with friends old and new, full of stories of the early days, of Uncas and other bygone people, and of the Pequot and King Philip's wars. Today that building is preserved as Leffingwell House Museum, a fit and proper memorial to Thomas Leffingwell, his descendants, and the early settlers of Norwich.

The final triumph of Thomas Leffingwell was to avoid probate taxes by distributing his estate to his children before he died. This was good for him and his children, but sad for history. A probate listing of his possessions would be interesting and helpful to better know and understand the man.

In his life Thomas Leffingwell served as a court-appointed appraiser to inventory the estates of people who had died, identifying and valuing their property and reporting it to the courts, where it was taxed. In August 1659 in Saybrook he had, with two others, taken inventory of the estate of Stephen Post, valuing it at 442. "This According to our best Light is a true Inventory of the Estate of Stephen Post of Seabrook, lately deceased," they reported to the court. He did the same for his neighbor across the street in Norwich, William Backus, in June1664.[194] There were probably several other times when this was done. It was a common service of men in the community.

Leffingwell began the process of deeding properties to his children as early as 1687, when he made, in part, a distribution of land to his oldest son Thomas. He gave him "fower parcells of land and meadow at Wequanack being part of my division land and part grant from the town." To his son Joseph he gave "two parcells over the river at Wequanuck." For the "land over the Shawtucket at the ferrie," he gave two thirds to his son Nathaniel and one-third to his son-in-law Robert Parke, the husband of his daughter, Rachel.

Leffingwell had land in the three towns of Norwich, Montville and Bozrah. It is said, doubtless with some exaggeration, that he "built five houses, one for each of his sons, these all within signaling distance of each other."[195] He gave George Rood, whom he had raised in his home after the infamous incest case of Thomas Rood, land for him and his new wife.

Mary Leffingwell preceded her husband in death, passing away on February 6, 1710/1711.[196] She lies buried in the Norwich Founder's Cemetery. Whether she was English or Mohegan, she had been the steady and longtime companion of Thomas Leffingwell. It is unfortunate that more is not known of her. They spent sixty three years together.

In September of 1714 Thomas Leffingwell, now ninety, made a last conveyance of his property. His son, Samuel, had died in 1691, leaving a grandson who was raised by Thomas and Mary. "In consideration of my comfortable maintainence dureing my naturall life, ... by my grandson Samuel Leffingwell," Thomas deeded him "all my home-lot that is not disposed of before thee date hereof, with thee Buildings upon it." The notarization on the deed by Richard Bushnell establishes that the old man was still alive. "Thomas Leffingwell personally appeared," Bushnell certified, "and acknowledged the above written instrument to be his own voluntary act and deed before me."[197]

This was the last known act of Thomas Leffingwell. We do not know just when he died. Four months later in January 1715 his son Thomas signed his name and left off the notation of "Jr.," indicating that he did not have a living father of the same name. It seems reasonable to believe that Thomas Leffingwell died sometime in the closing months of 1714.[198] He had lived in ten decades from the 1620s to the 1710s.

It seems strange, and is certainly unfortunate, that the death of one of the founders of the community went unrecorded in the Norwich town records. Many other deaths, among births and marriages, were well noted before and after his. Perhaps this hazy ending is simply poetic justice, a symmetry of nature. Seemingly from nowhere and without a past, Thomas Leffingwell appeared as a young man in the forests of Connecticut at the beginning of time in that state's history. Then, eighty years later, quietly and without fanfare, he simply disappears from our view.

He was buried in the Norwich Founders Cemetery, where all graves are today unmarked. There stands a large general monument, however, with the name "Mason" prominently at the bottom. Other names are on each face. At the top of one side are the words "Serg't Thos. Leffingwell."

Thomas Leffingwell lived a positive life of action. He did his duty on every front - as a husband and father, provider for his loved ones, a citizen of his community, surveyor of the wilderness, a church man, military soldier, public servant, and genuine friend to Uncas and the Mohegans. He was a man for all seasons. Thomas Leffingwell was a good man then, and after more than three hundred years, he stands as a good man now.

THE END

Appendix A

The Descendants of Thomas Leffingwell

In *The Leffingwell Record, 1637-1897*, Dr. Albert Leffingwell wrote that, "We should like to think it probable that a century hence, this record of the descendants of Lt. Thomas Leffingwell would be continued to his own time by some member of the family of that distant day." In partial fulfillment of that wish, the descendants of Thomas Leffingwell down to the author of this book, Russell Mahan, are as follows:

1. Thomas Leffingwell (1621/1625-1714) married Mary [possibly White, or Uncas] (c. 1630-1711)
2. Mary Leffingwell (1654-1745) m. Joseph Bushnell (1651-1746)
3. Nathan Bushnell (1686-1770) m. Mehitable Allen (1694-1750)
4. Samuel Bushnell (1721-1751) m. Zeriah Lyman (1723-1749)
5. Elijah Bushnell (1746-1843) m. Eunice Pratt (1750-1840)
6. Alvin Bushnell (1793-1874) m. Fanny Shepard (1797-1868)
7. Sarah Jane Bushnell (1834-1909) m. William Hall (1829-1878)
8. Flora Augusta Hall (1861-1954) m. Niceus Walker Mayginnes (1856-1926)
9. Marielva Mayginnes (1896-1980) m. Charles Smith Bledsoe (1892-1956)
10. Bettie Marie Bledsoe (1918-1985) m. Nibert Francis Mahan (1917-1992)
    11. Sharon Sue Mahan (b. 1941) m. James L. Haste
        12. James Mahan Haste (b. 1970)
    11. N F (Nibert Francis Jr.) Mahan (b. 1944) m. Karen Worth
        12. Sydney Mahan Befort (b. 1971)
        12. Daphne (Frostie) Mahan Peterson (b. 1975)
        12. Logan Gray Mahan (b. 1977)
    11. Marsha Lu Mahan (b. 1945) m. Don R. Devine
        12. Alan Mahan Devine (b. 1965)
        12. Mark Randall Devine (b. 1967)
        12. Dena Lyn Devine Kneisl (b. 1972)
    11. Russell Lee Mahan (b. 1951) m. Kami Garfield
        12. Jacob Russell Mahan (b. 1974)
        12. Mary Mahan (b. 1975)
        12. Katie Mahan Downs (b. 1984)
        12. Deidre Mahan Smith (b. 1990)

Appendix B

The Lands of Thomas Leffingwell

The lands of Thomas Leffingwell listed in the town records of Norwich, Connecticut:

1. "His home Lott twelve acres more or less, abuting northerly on Joseph Bushnells land seventeen rods, abuting westerly on the highway eighty six rods, abutting southeasterly on the land of Joseph Bushnell twenty rods, abutting easterly on his pasture land, being layd out November 1659."

2. "Ten acres of pasture land, abutting westerly on his home lott...."

3. "Nine acres...abutting east on the meadow of John Reynolds.... Seven acres of it first division laid out April 1661. Two acres purchased of John Reynolds."

4. "Four acres and an halfe of meadow... in Twenty Acre Meadow... abutting southerly on the Comons... abutting northerly on the highway, abutting easterly on the River... being part of the first division laid out Aprill 1661...."

5. "Twelve acres and an halfe over the River, abutting the highway... abutting on the river easterly eighty four rods, purchast of Christopher Huntington...."

6. "Sixty three acres...at Tradeing Cove...."

7. "Three acres...lyeing on top of Owanecoas Hill in the Little Plaine...."

8. "Fifty acres...on the point at Tradeing Cove, abutting on the River easterly one hundred and forty four rods.... A grant from the Town January 30, 1687."

9. "Twenty five acres... on the south side of the river at Wequanuck...."

10. "Two acres of upland and meadow on the west side of Shoutuckit River at the head of Wequanuck Island..."

11. "Five acres against Wequanuck Island, abutting the river southwesterly..."

12. "Ten acres of upland and meadow on the north side of the Little River...."

13. "Fifty one acres of land on the east side of Quenabauge River abutting the Brooke, northeast eighty rods to a white oake markt TL...."

14. "One hundred and fifty acres...lyeing on the east side of Quenabauge River, abutting southerly on Pachauge River...."

15. "Three acres of pasture land lying on the east side of the town...."

16. "Two acres and a quarter of pasture land.... abutting northwesterly on land of his son Thomas Leffingwell...."

17. "Four acres of pasture land on the east side of the long hill...."

18. "One hundred sixty and five acres of land upon the middle hill....

19. "Thirteen acres and an halfe of woodland... lying on the east side of the long hill brook...."

20. "Twenty six acres at the north end of the Great Plaine...."

21. "Seven acres and an halfe on the hill northward from the little fort...."

22. "Eighteen acres on the hill upon the east side of the great plaine...."

These twenty two lands total about 640 acres, or one square mile, of Connecticut countryside.

Appendix C

Surveying Assignments by the Colonial Legislature

Thomas Leffingwell was appointed by the colonial legislature of Connecticut, called the General Court, to do the following surveys:

- May 13, 1669. "Mr. Tho: Stanton and James Morgan are desired by this Court to lay out the land that was granted to Lnt James Avery," the record states, "and Tho: Leppingwell & Cristover Huntington to lay out to Lnt Francis Griswold what was granted to him."[199]

- May 9, 1672. "Ensign Tracy is appointed with Sergt. Thos. Leffingwell in layeing out to the Major [Mason] and Mr. Howkins their grants of lands according to their grants."[200]

- October 10, 1672. "This Court appoynts Ens: Tho: Leffingwell and Mr. Tho: Tracey to lay out to Mr. Haynes his children, the grant of land granted to them, according to their grant, at a place near Mr. Stanton's Farme, on the east side of Pawcatuck River."[201]

- October 10, 1672. "This Court appoynts Ens: Tho: Tracey and Ens: Tho: Leffingwell to lay out to Wm. Pratt his grant of land, according to his grant."[202]

- October 10, 1672. "This Court appoynts Ens: Tracey and Ens: Tho: Leffingwell to lay out to the towne of Stoneington their east bownds, according to their former grants from this Court.."[203]

- May 8, 1673. "This Court accepts the return of Ens: Tho: Tracey and Ens: Tho: Leffingwell concerning the laying out of the east bownds of Stoneington, and give them liberty to record the same in the Booke of records."[204]

- May 14, 1674. Leffingwell and two others were appointed to "lay out certain lands which were claimed within the bounds of Connecticut on the east side of the Pawtucket river, as having been given to Harvard College, but which had been encroached upon by the Rhode Island people."[205]

- May 14, 1674. "Mr. Math: Griswold, Lt Tho: Tracey and Ens: Thomas Leffingwell and Mr. Tho: Minor, they or any two or three of them are appoynted to lay out those lands accordingly, when called by the proprietors" of Stonington and New London.[206]

- October 8, 1674. "This Court doth appoynt Lt Tho: Tracey and Ens: Tho: Leffingwell to lay out to Major Edward Palmes his grant of land, according to his former grant, and to Mr. Samuel Stone or his assigne the remaynder of his grant according to his grant."[207]

- May 13, 1675. "This Court [appoints] Lnt Tho: Tracey and Ens: Tho: Leffingwell to lay out to the Reverend Mr. James Fitch, Lnt John Mason, Ens: John Standly and Mr. Daniel Witherell, their respective grants of land, according to their grants."[208]

- October 11, 1677. "This Court grants Jonathan Armstrong the sume of one hundred acres of land near the bownds of Norwich, provided he take it up where it may not prejudice any former grant to any plantation or perticuler person. Lnt Tho: Tracey and Lnt Tho: Leffingwell are appoynted to lay out his grant to him, according to his grant."[209]

- May 8, 1679. "This Court appoynts Mr. Tho: Tracey and Mr. Tho: Lefingwell to lay out to Mr. Amos Richeson a former grant of land to him according to his grant, and to Aron Start and to James Rogers... theire former grants of land according to their respective grants."[210]

- May 14, 1685. "This Court doe appoynt Lnt Thomas Leffingwell and Mr. Alexander Pygon to lay out to Samuel Rogers his grant of land granted to him by this Court, according to his grant."[211]

- May 14, 1685. "This Court appoynt Lnt Tho. Leffingwell and Capt. James Avery and Nehemiah Palmer, they or any two of them, to lay out and bownd the sundry parcells of land given to the Pequots, in New London or Stoneington bownds or lands adjacent."

- October 8, 1685. "Therefore this Court order Lnt Leffingwell and John Post to run the lyne afoarsayd... and that the sayd Leffingwell and Post see it sufficiently bownded, and cause the same to be recorded in the booke of recordes for land in Stoneington, as the... lyne of divission between the sayd Gallops and Denison."[212]

- October 10, 1695. "The return of Mr. Leffingwell and John Post about the running of Stoneington north bownds and Preston sowth bownds according to former order of Court, and the Court approves of the same and order it to be kept on file." This boundary description was quoted in full above.

- October 10, 1695. "Mr. John Bowcher and Mr. Leffingwell are to lay out to Giles Hamlin and Mr. Nath. Collins their grants of land according to their grants."[213]

Endnotes

1. Trumbull, Benjamin, *A Complete History of Connecticut, Civil and Ecclesiastical* (New London, CT: H.D. Utley, 1898), xv.

2. Leffingwell, Albert, and Leffingwell, Charles Wesley, *The Leffingwell Record, 1637-1897* (Aurora, NY: Leffingwell Publishing Company, 1897), 9.

3. Ibid., 11.

4. Comments of Mrs. Bela P. Learned, *Norwich Bulletin*, Norwich, CT, Tuesday, January 26, 1909, p. 5.

5. Deposition of Thomas Leffingwell, Leffingwell Family Collection, MSS 25, New Haven Historical Society collection.

6. Caulkins, Frances Manwaring, *History of Norwich, Connecticut; From Its Possession by the Indians to the Year 1866* (Hartford, CT: Published by the Author, 1866), 189.

7. Ibid., 189.

8. Leffingwell, 11.

9. Ibid., 10.

10. Ibid., 3-8.

11. Ibid., 10.

12. Floud, Roderick and Johnson, Paul Johnson, Editors, *The Cambridge Economic History of Modern Britain*, Vol. *I: Industrialisation, 1700-1860 (*Cambridge: University Press, 2004), 344.

13. Leffingwell, 10.

14. Oberg, Michael Leroy, *Uncas: First of the Mohegans* (Ithaca, NY: Cornell University Press, 2003), 37.

15. Grant, Marion Hepburn, *Fort Saybrook at Saybrook Point* (Centerbrook, CT: Old Saybrook Historical Society, 2016), 2.

16. Connecticut State Library / State Archives, Private Controversies 1642-1717, page 37b.

17. The Talcott Papers, Correspondence and Documents, *Collections of the Connecticut Historical Society, Volume 5* (Hartford, CT: Connecticut Historical Society, 1896), 198.

18. Trumbull, Benjamin, 44.

19. Stedman, John W., Editor, The Norwich Jubilee (Norwich, CT: John W. Stedman, 1859), 55.

20. Trumbull, Benjamin, 194.

21. Drake, Samuel G., *The Book of the Indians of North America* (Boston: Josiah Drake, 1838), 94.

22. *Genealogical and Biographical Record of New London County, Connecticut* (Chicago: J.H. Beers, 1905), 430.

23. Trumbull, Benjamin, 194-195.

24. Leffingwell, 14-15.

25. Drake, 94.

26. Caulkins, 40-41.

27. Trumbull, Benjamin, 194-195.

28. Caulkins, 40-41.

29. Leffingwell, 15.

30. Gilman, William G., *The Celebration of the 250th Anniversary of the Settlement of the Town of Norwich*, (Norwich, CT, Published by the Author, 1912), 35-36.

31. DeForest, John W., *History of the Indians fo Connecticut, Earliest Known Period to 1850* (Hartford, CT: Wm. Jas, Hamersley, 1852), 213.

32. Fawcett, Melissa Jane, "The Lasting of the Mohegans" (Ledyard, CT: The Mohegan Tribe, 1995), 14.

33. Caulkins, 43, footnote.

34. Leffingwell, 14-15.

35. Caulkins, 40.

36. Leffingwell, 15-16.

37. Caulkins, 41, DeForest, 214, Leffingwell Monument on the Mohegan Reservation.

38. Stone, William L., *Uncas and Miantonomoh*, New York: Dayton & Newman, 1842), 137.

39. Hollister, Gideon H., *The History of Connecticut from the First Settlement of the Colony to the Adoption of the Present Constitution* (Hartford, CT: The American Subscription House, 1855), 199; also Thatcher, B.B., *Indian Biography, Vol. I* (New York: Harper & Brothers, New York, 1836), 272.

40. Caulkins, 41.

41. Trumbull, Benjamin, 195.

42. Leffingwell, 9.

43. Main, Jackson Turner, *Society and Economy in Colonial Connecticut* (Princeton: Princeton University Press, 1985), 7.

44. Torrey, Clarence Almon, *New England Marriages Prior to 1700* (Baltimore: Genealogical Publishing Company, 1985), 460.

45. Caulkins, 189.

46. Leffingwell, 217.

47. Oberg, 81.

48. Buelle, Robert Rood, Editor, *The Rood-Rude Record*, a Family Genealogical Newsletter, Volume I, No. 3, Summer 1954, p. 53.

49. Torrey, 651.

50. Leffingwell, 14-15.

51. Leffingwell, 218.

52. Trumbull, Benjamin, 84.

53. Gates, Gilman C., *Saybrook at the Mouth of the Connecticut: The First One Hundred Years*, Press of the (New Haven, CT, Wilson H. Lee Company, 1935), 142.

54. Main, 200, 9.

55. Stedman, 165-166.

56. Gates, 97.

57. Grant, 17.

58. Gates, 132, 215.

59. Trumbull, J. Hammond, Compiler, *The Public Records of the Colony of Connecticut, Prior to the Union with New Haven Colony, May 1665* (Hartford: Brown & Parsons, 1850), 205-206.

60. Saybrook Town Records, page 25.

61. Trumbull, J. Hammond, *The Public Records of the Colony of Connecticut, Prior to 1665*, 218.

62. Chesebrough, Harriet Chapman, *Glimpses of Saybrook in Colonial Days* (Saybrook, CT: Celebration 3-1/2, 1985), 88.

63. *Records of the Particular Court of Connecticut 1639-1663* (Hartford, CT: Connecticut Historical Society, 1928), 145-146.

64. *The Code of 1650, Being a Compilation of the Earliest Laws and Orders of the General Court of Connecticut* (Hartford, CT: Silas Andrus,1822), 69.

65. "Massachusetts Marriage Ways: The Puritan Idea of Marriage as a Contract," Austin Community College, www.austincc.edu/jdikes/Marriage%20Ways%20ALL.pdf

66. *Vital Records of Saybrook 1647-1834*, (Hartford, CT: The Connecticut Historical Society, 1952), 6.

67. Leffingwell, 26.

68. Warner, Lucien C., *The Descendants of Andrew Warner* (New Haven, CT: Tuttle, Morehouse & Taylor Co., 1919), 73.

71. Chapman, Edward M., *The First Church of Christ, Old Saybrook, Conn., The Celebration of the 250th Anniversary, Wednesday, July 1, 1896*, (Middletown, CT: J.S. Stewart, 1896), 84-86.

70. Saybrook Town Records, 263.

71. Trumbull, Benjamin, 195.

72. Perkins, Mary E., *Old Houses of the Ancient Town of Norwich, 1660-1800* (Norwich, CT: Published by the Author, 1895), 5.

73. Stedman, 253.

74. Marshall, Benjamin Tinkham, Jr., *A Modern History of New London County, Connecticut, Volume I* (New York: Lewis Historical Publishing Company, 1922), 127

75. Perkins, 38.

76. Perkins, 62.

77. Leffingwell, 20.

78. Caulkins, 75.

79.Perkins, 39-40.

80. Ibid., 8.

81. Ibid., 8-9.

82. Ibid., 13.

83. Ibid., 21.

84. Ibid, 21-22.

85. Norwich Town Records, 24-26.

86. Marshall, Volume I, 126.

87. Leffingwell, 20.

88. Finlay, Nancy, "The Importance of Being Puritan: Church and State in Colonial Connecticut," ConnecticutHistory.Org.

89. Stedman, 126-127.

90. Leffingwell, 26, 33-35.

91. Perkins, 40.

92. Leffingwell, 26-36.

93. Trumbull, J. Hammond, *The Public Records of the Colony of Connecticut, Prior to 1665*, 389.

94. Trumbull, J. Hammond, Compiler, *Records of the Colony of Connecticut, 1665-1678*, 154-155.

95. *The Public Statute Laws of the State of Connecticut, Published by Authority of the General Assembly* (Hartford, CT: Hudson & Goodwin, 1808), Volume I, 356.

96. "The Oath of a Freeman," TeachingAmericanHistory.org.

97. Trumbull, J. Hammond, *Records of the Colony of Connecticut, 1665-1678*, 523.

98. Indians, 1647-1789, Connecticut State Library, 37b.

99. Perreault, Donald, *Saybrook's Witchcraft Trial of 1661* (Saybrook, CT: Old Saybrook Historical Society, 2013), 6.

100. *The Code of 1650, Being a Compilation of the Earliest Laws and Orders of the General Court of Connecticut*, Hartford, CT: Silas Andrus, 1830, 30.

101. Norman-Eady, Sandra, "Connecticut Witch Trials and Posthumous Pardons," December 18, 2006, Connecticut General Assembly Website, www.cga.ct.gov/2006/rpt/ 2006-R-0718.htm

102. Perreault, 7.

103. Ibid., 3.

104. Trumbull, J. Hammond, *The Public Records of the Colony of Connecticut, Prior to the Union with New Haven Colony, May 1665*, 338.

105. Hall, David D., Editor, *Witch-Hunting in Seventeenth Century New England, A Documentary History, 1638-1693,*

(Boston, MA: Northeastern University Press, 1991), 98.

106. Perreault, 20-21.

107. *Vital Records of Norwich*, Publication Committee, Society of Colonial Wars in the State of Connecticut, Hartford, 1913, 34.

108. Court of Assistants held at Hartford October 8, 1672.

109. Trumbull, J. Hammond, Compiler, *Records of the Colony of Connecticut, 1665-1678*, 184.

110. Ibid.

111. *Colonial New England Records, 1643-1702*, 53:99; Martin-Cowger, Alicia Desiree, "A Great Appearance of Force: Puritan Family Government in Colonial Connecticut, 1672-1725," Thesis, Boise State University, 2010, p. 63.

112. *Connecticut County Court, New London County, Records of Trials, 1661-1855, Volume III, June 1670 - June 1681* (Hartford, CT: Connecticut State Library, 1922), 108.

113. Caulkins, 250.

114. Ibid, 58-72.

115. Trumbull, J. Hammond, *The Public Records of the Colony of Connecticut, Prior to 1665*, 384-391.

116. Main, 322.

117. Trumbull, J. Hammond, *The Public Records of the Colony of Connecticut, Prior to 1665*, 410.

118. Ibid., 412.

119. Trumbull, J. Hammond, *Records of the Colony of Connecticut, 1665-1678*, 129.

120. Ibid., 239.

121. Ibid., 292.

122. Ibid, 139.

123. Ibid., 197-198.

124. Trumbull, J. Hammond, Compiler, *The Public Records of the Colony of Connecticut, 1678-1689* (Hartford: Press of Case, Lockwood & Company, 1859), 43.

125. Ibid., 156.

126. Trumbull, J. Hammond, Compiler, *Records of the Colony of Connecticut, 1665-1678*, 292.

127. Trumbull, J. Hammond, *The Public Records of the Colony of Connecticut, Prior to 1665*, 419.

128. Trumbull, J. Hammond, Compiler, *Records of the Colony of Connecticut, 1665-1678,* 93, 100.

129. Ibid., 314.

130. Hoadly, Charles *J., Compiler, The Public Records of the Colony of Connecticut, 1689-1706* (Hartford: Press of Case, Lockwood & Brainard, 1868), 153.

131. Trumbull, J. Hammond, *Records of the Colony of Connecticut, 1665-1678*, 94.

132. Ibid., 181.

133. Ibid.

134. Ibid., 207-208.

135. Schultz, Eric B., and Tougias, Michael J., *King Philips War* (New York: The Countryman Press, 1999), 5.

136. Caulkins, 107.

137. Caulkins, 107-108.

138. Trumbull, J. Hammond, *Records of the Colony of Connecticut, 1665-1678*, 416-418.

139. Stedman, 65.

140. Hubbard, William, *A Narrative of the Indian Wars in New-England, from the First Planting thereof in the Year 1607 to the year 1677* (Worcester, MA: Joseph Wilder, 1801), 186.

141. Trumbull, J. Hammond, *Records of the Colony of Connecticut, 1665-1678*, 427.

142. Schultz, 286-287.

143. Ellis, George W., and Morris, John E., *King Philip's War* (New York: The Grafton Press, 1906) 223.

144. Fraser, Rebecca, *The Mayflower: The Families, The Voyage, and the Founding of America* (New York: St. Martin's Press, 2017), 279.

145. Warren, Jason W., "Connecticut Unscathed: Victory in The Great Narragansett War (King Philip's War), 1675-1676," Thesis, Ohio State University 2011, p 263.

146. Trumbull, J. Hammond, *Records of the Colony of Connecticut, 1665-1678*, 284-285.

147. Ibid., 280.

148. Ibid., 281-283.

149. Trumbull, J. Hammond, Compiler, *Records of the Colony of Connecticut, 1665-1678*, 474.

150. Ibid., 296-298.

151. Hoadly, 186.

152. Bodge, George Madison, *Soldiers in King Philip's War*, (Boston, MA: Printed by the Author, 1906), 441-446. Also, Larned, Ellen D., *History of Windham County Connecticut, Volume I* (Worcester, MA: Published by the Author, 1874), 239-241.

153. Trumbull, J. Hammond, *The Public Records of the Colony of Connecticut, 1678-1689*, 60.

154. Trumbull, J. Hammond, *Records of the Colony of Connecticut, 1665-1678*, 305.

155. Trumbull, J. Hammond, *The Public Records of the Colony of Connecticut, 1678-1689*, 100.

156. Ibid., 107.

157. Ibid., 157.

158. Ibid., 205-206.

159. Hoadly, 99.

160. Trumbull, J. Hammond, *The Public Records of the Colony of Connecticut, 1678-1689*, 117.

161. Ibid., 172.

162. Trumbull, Benjamin, 205-206.

163. Trumbull, J. Hammond, *The Public Records of the Colony of Connecticut, 1678-1689*, 136-138.

164. Ibid., 179-180.

165. Ibid., 248.

166. Trumbull, Benjamin, 309.

167. Trumbull, J. Hammond, *The Public Records of the Colony of Connecticut, 1678-1689*, 250-251.

168. Hoadly, 31.

169. Ibid., 110.

170. Ibid., 323.

171. Ibid., 336.

172. Ibid., 351.

173. Ibid., 416-417.

174. *Norwich Record of Town Votes, Volume I. 1681-1722*, Meeting on May 20, 1689, Norwich Town Records.

175. Perkins, 2.

176. Caulkins, 125.

177. *Norwich Bulletin*, Norwich, CT, Thursday, June 23, 1921, p. 12.

178. Caulkins, 127.

179. Oberg, 201.

180. Ibid., 205.

181. Trumbull, J. Hammond, *The Public Records of the Colony of Connecticut, 1678-1689*, 55, footnote.

182. Stone, 201-202.

183. Caulkins, 261-262.

184. Trumbull, J. Hammond, *The Public Records of the Colony of Connecticut, 1678-1689*, 175-176.

185. Ibid., 170.

186. *Land Disputes Between the Colony of Connecticut and the Mohegans* (1740), 205.

187. Trumbull, Benjamin, 357.

188. *Land Disputes Between the Colony of Connecticut and the Mohegans* (1740), 205.

189. Caulkins, 189.

190. Leffingwell, 24-25.

191. British History Online, America and West Indies: August 1705, https://www.british-history.ac.uk/cal-state-papers/colonial/america-west-indies/vol22/pp600-613.

192. Trumbull, Benjamin, 358-359.

193. Caulkins, 269.

194. Manwaring, Charles William, Compiler, *A Digest of the Early Connecticut Probate Records, Volume I, Hartford District 1635-1700* (Hartford, CT: R.S. Pect & Company, Printers, 1904), 144.

195. Marshall, 56.

196. *Norwich Vital Records 1654-1811*, Norwich City Clerk's Office, pp. 30-31.

197. Perkins, 40.

198. Leffingwell, 25.

199. Trumbull, J. Hammond, *Records of the Colony of Connecticut, 1665-1678*, 113.

200. Ibid., 171.

201. Ibid., 187-188.

202. Ibid., 189.

203. Ibid.

204. Ibid., 196.

205. Leffingwell, 22.

206. Trumbull, J. Hammond, *Records of the Colony of Connecticut, 1665-1678*, 228.

207. Ibid., 240.

208. Ibid., 257.

209. Ibid., 324.

210. Trumbull, J. Hammond, *The Public Records of the Colony of Connecticut, 1678-1689*, 29.

211. Ibid., 171-172.

212. Ibid., 189.

213. Hoadly, 154.

Bibliography

Abbey, Matilda O., *Genealogy of the Family of Lt. Thomas Tracy of Norwich, Connecticut*, Milwaukee: D.S. Harkness & Co., 1889.

Adams, Charles Kendall, Editor, *The Universal Cyclopedia, Volume XII*, D. New York: Appleton & Company, 1900.

Allyn, Adeline Bartlett, *Black Hall: Traditions and Reminiscences*, Hartford: The Case, Lockwood & Brainard Company, 1908.

Arnold, James N., Editor, *The Narragansett Historical Register, Volume I, 1882-83*, Hamilton, RI: The Narragansett Historical Publishing Company, Hamilton, RI, 1883.

Baker, Henry A., *History of Montville, Connecticut, 1640 to 1896*, Hartford: The Case, Lockwood & Brainard Company, 1896. The account in this book of the rescue of Uncas by Thomas Leffingwell is completely unreliable and should be disregarded.

Banks, Charles Edward, *Topographical Dictionary of 2885 English Emigrants to New England, 1620-1650*, Philadelphia: Elijah Ellsworth Brownell, 1937.

Bayless, Richard M., *History of Windham County, Connecticut*, New York: W.W. Peeston & Co., 1889.

Bodge, George Madison, *Soldiers in King Philip's War*, Boston: Published by the Author, 1906.

Bremer, Francis J., *Puritanism: A Very Short Introduction*, New York: Oxford University Press, 2009.

Burgess, Kimberly G., and Spilde, Katherine A., *Indian Gaming and Community Building: A History of the Intergovernmental Relations of the Mohegan Tribe of Connecticut*, Harvard University, 2004.

Caulkins, Frances Manwaring, *History of Norwich, Connecticut, from Its Possession by the Indians to the Year 1866*, Norwich: Published by the Author, 1874.

Chesebrough, Harriet Chapman, *Glimpses of Saybrook in Colonial Days*, Saybrook: Celebration 3-1/2, 1985.

The Code of 1650, Being a Compilation of the Earliest Laws and Orders of the General Court of Connecticut, Hartford: Silas Andrus, 1822.

Collections of the Connecticut Historical Society, Volumes V (1896), XI (1907) and XIV (1912), Hartford: Connecticut Historical Society.

Connecticut Historical Society, Waterman Research Center, Hartford, Connecticut.

Connecticut State Library / State Archives, Hartford,, Connecticut.
- Miscellaneous Papers 1635-1789
- Civil Officers 1669-1756
- Colonial Boundaries 1662-1827
- War 1675-1775
- Ecclesiastical Affairs 1658-1789
- Indians 1647-1789, Second Series 1666-1820
- NLCC Native American Cases
- Private Controversies 1642-1717
- Towns and Lands 1629-1789
- Towns and Lands, 2nd Series, May 1649-May 1820
- Travel and Taverns, 1700-1788

Contemporary American Biography, Volume III, New York: Atlantic Publishing and Engraving Company, 1902.

De Forest, John W., *History of the Indians of Connecticut: from the Earliest Known Period to A.D. 1850*, Hartford: Wm. Jas. Hamersley, 1851.

Drake, Samuel Adams, *Nooks and Corners of the New England Coast*, New York: Harper & Brothers, 1875.

Drake, Samuel G., *The Book of the Indians of North America*, Boston: Josiah Drake, 1838.

Fawcett, Melissa Jane, "The Lasting of the Mohegans," Ledyard, CT, The Mohegan Tribe, 1995.

Field, David D., *A Statistical Account of the County of Middlesex in Connecticut*, Middletown: Connecticut Academy of Arts and Sciences, 1819.

The First Church of Christ, Compiler, *Old Saybrook: The Celebration of the 250th Anniversary*, Middletown, CT: J.S. Stewart, 1896.

Gates, Gilman C., *Saybrook at the Mouth of the Connecticut: The First One Hundred Years*, New Haven: Published by the Author, 1935.

Genealogical and Biographical Record of New London County, Connecticut, Chicago: J.H. Beers & Co., 1905.

Gilman, William G., *The Celebration of the 250th Anniversary of the Settlement of the Town of Norwich*, Norwich, 1912.

Grant, Marion Hepburn, *Fort Saybrook at Saybrook Point*, Centerbrook, CT: Old Saybrook Historical Society, 1985, 2016.

Hall, David D., Editor, *Witch-Hunting in Seventeenth Century New England, A Documentary History, 1638-1693*, Boston: Northeastern University Press, 1991.

Hollister, Gideon H., *The History of Connecticut from the First Settlement of the Colony to the Adoption of the Present Constitution*, Hartford: The American Subscription House, 1855.

Hurd, D. Hamilton, Editor, *History of New London County, Connecticut*, Philadelphia: J.B. Lippincott & Co., 1882.

Jacobus, Donald Lines, *The Waterman Family, Volume I*, New Haven: Edgar F. Waterman, 1939.

Larned, Ellen D., *History of Windham County, Connecticut, Volume 1*, Worcester. MA: Published by the Author, 1874.

Leffingwell, Albert, and Leffingwell, Charles Wesley, *The Leffingwell Record, 1637-1897*, Aurora, NY: The Leffingwell Publishing Company, 1897.

Leffingwell House Museum Papers, Norwich, Connecticut.

Lester, William, Jr., *A Sketch of Norwich: including Notes of a Survey of the Town*, Norwich: J. Dunham, 1833.

Lossing, Benson J., *The Pictorial Field-Book of the Revolution, Volume II*, New York: Harper & Brothers, 1852.

Main, Jackson Turner, *Society and Economy in Colonial Connecticut*, Princeton: Princeton University Press, 1985.

Marshall, Benjamin Tinkham, Editor, *A Modern History of New London County, Connecticut*, New York: Lewis Historical Publishing Company, 1922.

Martin-Cowger, Alicia Desiree, "A Great Appearance of Force: Puritan Family Government in Colonial Connecticut, 1672-1725," Thesis, Boise State University, 2010.

The New England Historical and Genealogical Register, Volume VIII, Boston: Samuel G. Drake, 1854.

New Haven Historical Society Papers, Leffingwell Family Collection, MSS 25, New Haven, New Haven, Connecticut.

Norwich City Clerk's Records, Norwich, Connecticut.

Oberg, Michael Leroy, *Uncas: First of the Mohegans*, Ithaca, NY: Cornell University Press, 2003.

Old Saybrook Town Clerk's Records, Old Saybrook, Connecticut.

Old Saybrook Historical Society Collection, Old Saybrook, Connecticut.

Otis Library Genealogical Collection, Norwich, Connecicut.

Paine, Lyman May, *My Ancestors: A Memorial of John Paine and Mary Ann May*, Chicago: Published by Author, 1914.

Papers of the New Haven Historical Society, Volume III, New Haven: New Haven Colony Historical Society, 1882.

Peale, Arthur L., *Memorials and Pilgrimages in the Mohegan Country*, The Norwich: Bulletin Co., 1930.

Perkins, Mary E., *Old Houses of the Ancient Town of Norwich, 1660-1800*, Norwich: Published by the Author, 1895.

Perreault, Donald, *Saybrook's Witchcraft Trial of 1661*, Old Syabrook: Old Saybrook Historical Society, 2012.

Porter, George S., *Inscriptions from Gravestones in the Old Burying Ground, Norwich Town, Connecticut*, Norwich: The Nulletin Press, 1933.
The Public Records of the Colony of Connecticut:
- Trumbull, J. Hammond, Compiler -
- *The Public Records of the Colony of Connecticut, Prior to the Union with New Haven Colony, May 1665*, Hartford: Brown & Parsons, 1850.
- *The Public Records of the Colony of Connecticut, 1665-1678*, Hartford: F. A. Brown, 1852.
- *The Public Records of the Colony of Connecticut, 1678-1689*, Hartford: Press of Case, Lockwood & Company, 1859.
- Hoadly, Charles J., Compiler, *The Public Records of the Colony of Connecticut, 1689-1706*, Hartford: Press of Case, Lockwood & Brainard, 1868.

Railton, Stephen, *Fenimore Cooper: A Study of His Life and Imagination*, Princeton: Princeton University Press, 1978.

Records of the Particular Court of Connectciut, 1639-1663, Hartford: Connecticut Historical Society, 1928.

Schultz, Eric B., and Tougias, Michael J., *King Philip's War: The History and Legacy of America's Forgotten Conflict*, New York: The Countryman Press, 2017.

Sparks, Jared, Editor, *The Library of American Biography, Second Series, Volume III*, Boston: Charles C. Little & James Brown, 1844.

Stedman, John W., Editor, *The Norwich Jubilee*, Norwich: Published by the Editor, 1859.

Stone, William L., *Uncas and Miantonomoh: A Historical Discourse*, New York: Dayton & Newman, 1842.

"Summary Under the Criteria and Evidence for Final Determination in Regard to Federal Acknowledgement of the Paucautuck Eastern Pequot Indians of Connecticut as a Portion of the Historical Eastern Pequot Tribe," U.S. Department of the Interior, 2002.

Sweeney, Mary E., Bishop, Alice, and Avery, Rhoda, "History of Bozrah," 1916.

Swift, Ruth, *A History of the Village and the First Congregational Church of Windham, Connecticut*, Windham: 1975.

Sylvester, Herbert Milton, *Indian Wars of New England*, Boston: W.B. Clarke Company, 1910.

Thatcher, B.B., *Indian Biography, Volume I*, New York: Harper & Brothers, 1836.

Tomlinson, R.G., *Witchcraft Trials of Connecticut*, Hartford: The Bond Press, Inc., 1978.

Torrey, Clarence Almon, *New England Marriages Prior to 1700*, Baltimore: Genealogical Publishing Company, 1985,

Tracy, Evert E., *Tracy Genealogy: Ancestors and Descendants of Lieutenant Thomas Tracy of Norwich, Conn., 1660*, Albany: Joel Munsell's Sons, 1898.

Trumbull, Benjamin, *A Complete History of Connecticut, Civil and Ecclesiastical, from the Emigration of Its First Planters From England in the Year 1630 to the Year 1764*, New London: H. D. Utley, 1898.

Trumbull, Henry, *History of the Discovery of America*, Boston: George Clark, 1830.

Trumbull, J,. Hammond, *The Public Records of the Colony of Connecticut, Prior to May 1665*, Hartford: , Brown & Parsons, 1850) 218-220.

Tyler, Sarah Lester, *Norwich: Early Homes and History*, Norwich: Faith Trumbull Chapter D.A.R., 1906.

The Uncas Monument, Memorial Publication, 1842.

Vital Records of Norwich, Hartford: Publication Committee, Society of Colonial Wars in the State of Connecticut, 1913.

Vital Records of Saybrook, 1647-1834, Hartford: The Connecticut Historical Society, 1952.

Walters, Mark D., "Mohegan Indians v. Connecticut (1705-1773) and the Legal Status of Aboriginal Customary Laws and Government in British North America," Osgoode Hall law Journal 33.4 (1995) 785-829.

Walworth, Reuben Hyde, *Hyde Genealogy, or, The descendants, in the Female as well as in the Male lines, from William Hyde, of Norwich*, Albany: J. Munsell, Albany, 1864.

Warner, Lucien C., and Josephine Genung Nichols, Compilers, *The Descendants of Andrew Warner*, New Haven: The Tuttle, Morehouse & Taylor Co., 1919.

Wells, Hariette Hyde, *Several Ancestral Lines of Moses Hyde and his Wife Sarah Dana*, Albany: Johl Munsell's Sons, 1904.

Williams, Catherine, *Fall River, An Authentic Narrative*, Providence: Brown & Co., 1834.

Yale Manuscripts & Archives, Leffingwell Family Papers, MS 320, Box 1, Folder 1, Sterling Library, New Haven, Connecticut.

Index

Made in the USA
Middletown, DE
04 January 2023